HUNTING FOR "DIRTBAGS"

HUNTING FOR
"DIRTBAGS"

Why Cops Over-Police the Poor and Racial Minorities

LORI BETH WAY AND RYAN PATTEN

NORTHEASTERN UNIVERSITY PRESS | BOSTON

This book is dedicated to those who made it possible: Clare Renzetti, Susan Miller, and the wonderful people at UPNE. Most of all, this book would have been impossible without the support and cooperation of the Stonesville and Seaside Police Departments. We value their effort and assistance and we hope to have portrayed them fairly.

Northeastern University Press
An imprint of University Press of New England
www.upne.com
© 2013 Northeastern University
All rights reserved

Manufactured in the United States of America
Designed by April Leidig
Typeset in Arno by Copperline Book Services, Inc.

University Press of New England is a member of the Green Press Initiative. The paper used in this book meets their minimum requirement for recycled paper.

For permission to reproduce any of the material in this book, contact Permissions, University Press of New England, One Court Street, Suite 250, Lebanon NH 03766; or visit www.upne.com

Library of Congress Cataloging-in-Publication Data
Way, Lori Beth.
Hunting for "dirtbags" : why cops over-police the poor and racial minorities / Lori Beth Way and Ryan Patten.
    pages   cm
Includes bibliographical references and index.
ISBN 978-1-55553-812-5 (cloth : alk. paper)
ISBN 978-1-55553-813-2 (pbk. : alk. paper)
ISBN 978-1-55553-814-9 (ebook)
1. Police discretion. 2. Police-community relations.
3. Poor. 4. Minorities. 5. Police — United States —
Case studies. I. Patten, Ryan. II. Title.
HV7936.D54W39 2013
363.2'3080973 — dc23   2012048404

5 4 3 2 1

CONTENTS

HUNTING FOR "DIRTBAGS"

CHAPTER ONE

THE UNDIAGNOSED PROBLEM

Discretionary Proactive Policing

You can't hunt in nice neighborhoods.
— Stonesville officer

hat role should the police serve in a democratic society? Should police departments work to reduce crime and catch lawbreakers, or should their focus primarily be on responding to citizen calls for service or assistance? Of course, these strategies are not mutually exclusive, but one relies on police officers to ferret out crime and the other requires residents to report problems including crimes. As an example, for about the last fifteen years the New York Police Department (NYPD) has adopted a very aggressive strategy to attack crime by catching would-be criminals before they commit crime (also known as order maintenance or zero tolerance policing). During those fifteen years, New York City, and the rest of the nation in general, has witnessed declining crime rates, and in New York City, the reduced crime rate has been attributed to the assertive policing techniques of the NYPD. The NYPD's crime-fighting strategies, however, have had negative impacts as well; these have been exclusively concentrated in the Black and Latino neighborhoods of New York City. The practice of proactive policing and the damaging consequences of this policing tactic for racial minorities and those living in poverty are not new and are still prevalent around the nation. We will discuss some of these negative impacts and New York City Mayor Michael Bloomberg's cavalier response to them in detail later.

There is a long and well understood disconnect between how the police view their role and the day-to-day realities of their job. Whether desirable or not, police officers see themselves as crime fighters and want to be considered as such (Bittner 1990; Brown 1981; Klockars 1985; Manning 2001; Paoline 2004; Parnaby and Leyden 2011; Sparrow, Moore, and Kennedy 1990; Stanko 1989; Van Maanen 1974; Westley 1970). Research shows that approximately one-third of an officer's time is spent on law enforcement activities (Famega 2005, 2009). In fact, 70 to 80 percent of calls for service to police departments are basic order maintenance or service calls rather than incidents involving any criminal behavior (National Research Council 2004). The image of the job of a crime fighter, however, is one that centers on officers investigating and following up on their suspicions through traffic stops and other contacts.

During a ten-hour shift, patrol officers respond to a variety of different requests for service from the citizenry via emergency (9-1-1) calls. Depending on the size and location of the police jurisdiction, during that shift dispatchers may not send an officer to any calls for service or, in a busy area, may send an officer to dozens of calls. Even for busy districts, though, officers will have time that is unassigned. While the amount of that time will vary, police officers' unassigned time can reach three-quarters of their shift; how officers spend that time is completely discretionary (Famega, James, and Mazerolle 2005). What they choose to do with their "free time," and the implications of those choices, are the stories of this book and some of the biggest concerns with policing in America.

Enforcing laws is one component of the larger criminal justice system. Police officers work within that system and respond to its institutional incentives and constraints. Since the 1980s, criminologists have argued that the criminal justice system has become a set of institutions with a single goal, which focuses on punishment (Currie 1990; Gibbons 2000; Steen and Bandy 2007). There is no illusion of rehabilitation or reform, but rather a belief that retribution or deterrence is the means to reducing crime. Furthermore, some criminologists argue that the motive behind the tough-on-crime movement, or "new penology," is to increase the surveillance and perpetual containment of the poor (Feeley and Simon 1992; Pettit and Western 2004; Simon 1993; Western 2006) without having any positive effect on the crime rate (see Fagan and Meares 2008).[1] Additionally, increased incarceration of the poor and racial minorities actually creates long-term harm in these communities (Clear 2007; Pratt 2009). This book illustrates how the police fit into this larger political system. Specifically, through discretionary proactive policing (done in their "free time"), law enforcement officers monitor the lower classes to a greater degree than the middle and upper classes. Such police behavior feeds the cycle of depositing the poor into the criminal justice system and ensuring they remain under criminal justice scrutiny.

This research began with the following questions: What factors influence a police officer's discretionary decisions? How and why do officers make the decisions they do on the street? To what degree do police officers differ in their decision making and what explains that variability? Alternatively, do patrol officers act in ways that are similar? If the criminal justice system has particular goals to control a certain segment of the population, how do the police react to that political context?

The central arguments of this book include the following: (1) there are institutional and organizational structures and incentives within both the police department and the criminal justice process that induce officers to patrol the poor, especially those from racial and ethnic minorities, to a greater degree; and (2) the institutional goal to produce citations and arrests leads officers to proactively patrol. Note that both of these arguments are addressing the effects of institutional incentives and organizational structures. We often want a simple story. Cops are good. Cops are bad. Cops are bigots or racists. Cops are not bigots or racists. The truth about policing and police officers, however, is extraordinarily complex. While individual personalities have been shown to affect police behavior to some degree (Miller 2003; Skolnick 1966), institutional choices made by police and city leaders and professional expectations of officers constrain some behaviors and incentivize others.

The term *proactive policing* has been used by police scholars to refer to a variety of activities, often positively associated with field interrogations, traffic stops, and/or enforcing laws related to driving under the influence, loitering, or possession and public consumption of drugs and alcohol. When we use the term *proactive policing* in this book, however, we are not referencing specific organized police mobilizations to certain neighborhoods derived from crime reports, such as hot spot or COMPSTAT policing. In hot spot and COMPSTAT policing, the police response is organized at the administrative level and carried out by the officers with specific goals of reducing a particular type of crime (Bowers et al. 2011; Braga, Hureau, and Papachristos 2012; Maple and Mitchell 1999; Ratcliffe et al. 2011; Sherman and Weisburd 1995; Telep and Weisburd 2012; Timoney 2010; Weisburd and Eck 2004; Weisburd et al. 2003; Willis, Mastrofski, and Weisburd 2007). Both hot spot and COMPSTAT can be considered proactive policing, because both strategies rely on reported crime and previous proactive resident contacts.

The focus of this book, instead, is proactive policing at the individual, discretionary level. The officers describe proactive policing as any action an officer takes in order to identify a crime (or potential crime) committed, rather than relying on a citizen or victim reporting some sort of unwanted behavior. These officers are not following a specific crime reduction strategy as devised by the administration, but are simply contacting "suspicious" people and trying to catch would-be lawbreakers. This is also what officers in some jurisdictions call "hunting" and is almost exclusively practiced concerning visible crimes (for example, possession or selling of drugs, prostitution, and carrying guns; officers informally refer to people engaged in these activities as "dirtbags" or "scumbags"). Due to Fourth Amendment restrictions, offenses committed behind closed doors are almost impossible to hunt. We find here that proactive work, or hunting, by officers is almost exclusively done within economically poor neighborhoods — where racial minorities are more likely to be found. The result is racial minorities are subject to a greater level of surveillance than their White counterparts. As we discuss more thoroughly later, officers can spend up to 25 percent of their shifts engaged in hunting.

This claim is not new. There have been many authors who have argued that racial minorities experience a greater level of surveillance than Whites (Chambliss 1984; Harris 1999; Ruddell, Thomas, and Patten 2010; Russell 1998; Weitzer 2010); this is deeply familiar to minorities themselves (see Glover 2008). Questions regarding how and why this greater level of surveillance actually occurs have often been left unanswered, with the exception of discussions of racial profiling. Our research is a step toward understanding the *process* that results in a greater policing of minorities. The reason racial minority communities become more policed than White communities is that officers "hunt" for infractions or crimes within economically disadvantaged sections of a city because officers think these sections are where lawbreakers can easily be located. In Chapter 5, we will also see how probationers and parolees are policed to a greater degree and, therefore, policing of the poor is increased because those people on probation or parole are most often low-income or no-income individuals.

Ethnographies written by current and former police officers help highlight the concerns of discretionary proactive policing and discuss why it is viewed as practical and is so ingrained in officers. Officers *want* to hunt, *want* to find the "bad guys," and *want* to make arrests. They view these roles as the main part of their job, if not the only part of their job, and their administrations either support this effort or are indifferent to it.

Los Angeles police officer William Dunn wrote a book about his rookie, or "boot," year on the force. He stated in part, "LAPD [Los Angeles Police Department] officers are trained to get in their black-and-white [cars] and go looking for potential trouble ... LAPD officers scour their areas for suspicious persons or scenarios. This is called *proactive policing*" (emphasis in original; 2008, 42). In reference to how he patrolled, Dunn wrote that he and other LAPD officers would stop or "jam" suspicious people or people in suspicious situations, trying to evaluate if a crime had occurred or was about to occur. Later Dunn stated, "[b]asically the same knuckleheads do your street crimes over and over. So if you know the knuckleheads, and where they've been and who they hang out with and what they drive, you can solve [a lot] of crimes" (43). Dunn's passages create an interesting question for the critical reader: if LAPD officers know who the bad guys are, where they live, what they drive, and who they hang out with, and they're the ones committing most (if not all) of the street crimes, why would an officer "jam" other people? It would appear that in hopes of stumbling onto a criminal or a crime-fighting opportunity, officers are harassing and irritating innocent civilians who are creating no harm and breaking no laws. One officer employing this proactive technique can create a problem; an entire department dedicated to this strategy is sure to confuse and alienate those deemed to be "suspicious," which in the United States are those who are economically poor and racial minorities.

Dale Carson, a former Miami police officer who set felony arrest records for the state of Florida, wrote about his (and other's) attitudes about proactive policing. Carson stated in part, "[w]hat you've got to understand is this: cops *like* to hunt and pursue. They *enjoy* arresting people . . . The animal cops hunt is that prince of prey, the two-legged beast" (emphasis in original; 2007, 51). Carson continued talking about the strategy of hunting human beings, noting in part, "[c]ops crave variety and excitement . . . On slow days they can make their own excitement because they can always find someone to arrest. I call the technique 'flushing rabbits'" (53). Many might balk at Carson's rather insulting view of his fellow humans as "prey" and "rabbits."

Peter Moskos wrote about his year serving as a Baltimore police officer and about the administration's, as well as other officers', attitudes toward writing citations and making arrests. Moskos claimed in part, "officers believe that making arrests *is* police work" (emphasis in original; 2008, 137). More importantly, Moskos noted the institutional need for patrol officers to make arrests in order to be promoted into specialized (and more glamorous) units. "These [specialized] units are not always easy to get into. In some ways they are invitation only. But specialized units are also self-selective. Only some officers want to be on the narcotics squad, usually young, aggressive, high-arrest officers" (137). What Moskos revealed is known throughout the nation's police agencies: those officers who fight crime, who write a lot of tickets, and who make a lot of arrests are more likely to be considered come promotion time. Officers feel pressure to write citations and make arrests because that is what their superior officers and their administration demand. Our intention here is not to demonize police officers, but to expose how officers are driven to hunt in an attempt to produce citations and arrests that will appease the administration.

Officers work within organizational rules and philosophies,

but their activities on the streets are largely unsupervised, which grants them a great deal of individual discretion. The criminal justice system at all levels is a series of discretionary decisions that ultimately affects the liberty of individuals and the safety of citizens. A certain level of officer discretion is desirable and necessary. Given the voluminous nature of the penal and traffic codes, it is impossible for police officers to enforce all the laws, all the time. They must make choices. In this book, we explore the choices officers on the street make, the factors that influence them, and the implications of their decisions. Specifically, we consider discretion broadly, including discretionary choices of officers regarding their personal policing styles and priorities on the job. Instead of merely focusing on officers' use of discretion when interacting with the public, we also consider choices officers make regarding what type of officer they want to be and how they go about making the result of those choices a reality.

The trend for researchers and some policy makers has been to recommend that police departments focus on order maintenance, contending that such a strategy will reduce crime and build better relations with communities.[2] Order maintenance activities are rarely those considered by police to be the work of crime fighters. In addition, these activities — ticketing residents for graffiti on their homes, abandoned cars, or being drunk in public — are not the tasks officers usually relish.

The argument for a concentration on order maintenance first came into public and government consciousness with a now famous article entitled "Broken Windows" (Wilson and Kelling 1982). The main thesis is that neighborhoods appearing neglected or beginning to deteriorate will invite fear and crime. The authors contend that a New Jersey precinct that put officers on street corners on foot and had them enforce infractions and misdemeanors like vandalism and loitering did not see a reduction in crime, but did witness increased feelings of resident security. Wilson and Kelling argue that police departments should focus on disorder in order to reduce crime and increase the quality of life in communities (see also Kelling and Coles 1996; Skogan 1990; Xu, Fiedler, and Flaming 2005). Their article was the precursor to two large bodies of literature assessing and arguing for what have come to be termed *community policing* and *order maintenance policing*. For our purposes, we will focus more on order maintenance policing than community policing.

Order maintenance, at times under the guise of community policing, necessarily calls for a high degree of proactive policing. Garland (2001, 169) has commented on the link between community policing and proactive policing by writing, "in the policing sector, there has been a shift of emphasis away from reactive strategies and '911' policing, toward more proactive community policing efforts, and, more recently, to the more intensive policing of disorder, incivilities and misdemeanors" (see also Fagan et al. 2010; Geller and Fagan 2010; Golub, Johnson, and Dunlap 2007; Johnson, Golub, and McCabe 2010). In many high crime areas, where people think order maintenance is especially warranted, it is unlikely that citizens will report instances of vandalism, loitering, or public drunkenness. Given the unwillingness to report disorder, police officers are left to identify such actions for enforcement, and they are likely to identify them in particular types of people. As Fogelson noted decades ago (1977), the poor and minorities are more often on the streets and are, therefore, more likely to be scrutinized by patrol officers (see also Websdale 2001). Perhaps even more problematic is that residents do not actually seem to perceive disorder and crime as fundamentally different from one another. If people do not see these as distinct phenomena, then arguing that a rise in perceived disorder in a community leads to increased crime rests on an empirically unsound premise (Gau and Pratt 2008).

Successful Proactive Policing Strategies

As will become more apparent, our argument is not that all proactive policing strategies are inherently evil or should be eliminated. On the contrary, targeted proactive policing strategies, such as hot spot or COMPSTAT, have demonstrated the ability to reduce criminal activity in crime-ridden areas (Bowers et al. 2011; Braga et al. 2012; Braga and Bond 2008; Crisp and Hines 2007; Guerette and Bowers 2009; Moore and Braga 2003; Ratcliffe et al. 2011; Sherman and Weisburd 1995; Taylor, Koper, and Woods 211; Weisburd et al. 2006). Hot spot policing began with the idea of increased patrol in select areas of town known for "hard" crime calls (including physical violence and significant property crimes) and "soft" crime calls (including noise, loitering, and vandalism; Sherman and Weisburd 1995). A small number of addresses are typically responsible for a majority of "hard" and "soft" crime calls in any given city.

As explained by Sherman and Weisburd (1995), generally, a hot spot would be identified by the volume of calls to a very small geographic area—the hot spot would be confined to a linear block, and one hot spot could not be adjacent to another. After identifying the hot spot, the police department administration would devise an intervention strategy, typically patrol saturation. Based on the city's criminogenic patterns, a hot spot would only receive police intervention between 11:00 A.M. and 3:00 A.M. Additionally, each hot spot would receive steady patrol coverage for three hours a day and police would spend more patrol time in these hot spots (about twelve to fifteen minutes per hot spot). It is important to note that not all departments that practice hot spot policing do it in the exact same way. What Sherman and Weisburd, as well as others (Jang, Hoover, and Joo 2010; Ratcliffe et al. 2011; Weisburd and Eck 2004;

Weisburd and Lum 2005) noted was that crime rates were reduced at the hot spots after the police intervention. Similar to hot spot policing, COMPSTAT is a data-driven police response to crime. Started in the mid-1990s in New York City under Commissioner Bratton, COMPSTAT was a drastic change from the traditional reaction to crime (Bratton and Knobler 1998). Like hot spot policing, COMPSTAT was a strategic management system that used four elements: (1) accurate and timely crime data; (2) effective problem solving tactics; (3) focused resource deployment to implement those tactics; and (4) consistent follow-up and assessment to understand the intervention's success (McDonald 2004; Moore and Braga 2003; Timoney 2010; Walsh and Vito 2004; Willis, Mastrofski, and Weisburd 2003; 2007). In New York City, COMPSTAT was used in visible "Crime Control Strategy Meetings" to discuss the successfulness of crime reduction strategies (Weisburd et al. 2003). Perhaps the biggest change in the approach of COMPSTAT was the rate at which managers were receiving and incorporating fresh crime data. Instead of using data that was three to six months old and trying to look for trends, COMPSTAT used data from the previous week. Much like hot spot policing, COMPSTAT has been empirically tested in various cities, including, but not limited to New York City, New Orleans, Fort Worth, and Columbia, South Carolina, with all tests sites resulting in lower crime rates (Crisp and Hines 2007; Jang et al. 2010; Maple and Mitchell 1999; Weisburd et al. 2003; Willis et al. 2003).

While effective to a certain degree, hot spot policing and COMPSTAT are not a panacea nor are they able to reduce all types of crime in all areas. Our argument does not attempt to limit or eliminate hot spot policing, COMPSTAT, or any other empirically driving proactive policing. Both hot spot policing and COMPSTAT differ from our description and understanding of discretionary proactive policing in two key areas: they are empirically driven, and they are organized, department-wide crime reduction strategies.

Hunting for "Dirtbags" looks at the implications of *discretionary* proactive policing, focusing on the choices officers make when engaging in this optional practice and its effects on different communities and people. When on general patrol, officers choose to target a "shitty" neighborhood based on a hunch, anecdotal past experience, rumors, or something other than a confirmed empirically based reason. Additionally, these officers are not responding to a department-wide crime reduction strategy to focus on a certain block or neighborhood; instead, they are patrolling wherever they feel like simply because they want to or, more likely, because they feel pressure from the administration to produce numbers or "stats" (contacts, tickets, and arrests).

Discretionary proactive policing is also different from responding to community appeals that they would like more police presence or a greater focus on reducing narcotics sales. In those particular cases, residents are requesting police action. As a result of those requests, the police department might generate a hot spot program or analyze the community's needs using COMPSTAT data and then devise a plan in consultation with community members, strengthening police-community relations through this collaboration. *Discretionary* proactive policing, on the other hand, focuses on poor and minority communities and has had significant negative consequences for police-community relations.

The officers we observed and interviewed were not designated community policing or problem-oriented (for example, hot spot) policing officers. They were "regular" patrol officers (with the exception of the "6 squads," which are discussed later) who practiced discretionary proactive behavior that was indicative of what is proposed by advocates of aggressive order maintenance. Additionally, neither of the cities we observed was engaged in a comprehensive, department-wide COMPSTAT policing model. Aggressive order maintenance has the effect of undermining community relationships, but it is, nevertheless, often adopted by departments claiming to practice community policing. The idea of increased surveillance of downtrodden communities fits much more with the vision of a police officer as a crime fighter than the idea of going to a community's monthly meeting to assess the priorities of that neighborhood.

Proactive policing appears to support the larger goals of the current criminal justice system — goals which have changed in recent decades. While prior to the 1980s, the system was focused either on punishing or rehabilitating offenders, the new orientation focuses on managing or regulating individuals deemed socially undesirable or dangerous (Feeley and Simon 1992; Pettit and Western 2004; Western 2006). A large number of people are currently under criminal justice supervision and are cycling between incarceration and community corrections programs, such as probation and parole. As of 2010, the United States had 7.1 million adults under correctional supervision — 1 in 33 adults (Bureau of Justice Statistics 2011), which gave the United States the highest imprisonment rate of any country on the planet. *Hunting for "Dirtbags"* helps explain how the police play a role in regulating the behavior of the underclasses by maintaining an active presence in lower income areas.

Discretionary Proactive Contacts

In his seminal text on the police, Wilson (1968) noted that different police organizations promote different styles of policing — legalistic, watchman, and service — and that the administration sets the framework by which officers operate. In fact, Wilson stated in part that "the defining characteristic of the patrolman's role thus becomes the style or strategy of the department as a whole because it is reinforced by the attitudes and policies of the police administrator" (140). Research has supported the notion that the police organization reflects the influence of arrests (Black 1980; Eitle and Monahan 2009; Eitle, Stolzenberg, and D'Alessio 2005). Simply stated, officers feel pressure to perform well on indicators that their administration values.

The legalistic style of policing introduced by Wilson aligns with the traditional crime fighter view, where the police are supposed to make arrests and lock up the "bad guys," while ignoring or minimizing service requests. The fact that police view themselves as crime fighters has long been supported in the literature (Bittner 1990; Brown 1981; Klockars 1985; Manning 2001; Paoline 2004; Parnaby and Leyden 2011; Sparrow, Moore, and Kennedy 1990; Stanko 1989; Van Maanen 1974; Westley 1970). While different police administrations can have differing views about their role in society, a police administration with a crime fighter ideology will easily sway officers to this philosophy too. Retired Seattle Police Chief Norm Stamper provided excellent insight into how the administration's policies influence the daily activities of its officers. Stamper recalled how, when he was a young officer in the San Diego Police Department, it was expected that each officer complete five stop-and-frisk contacts, write two traffic citations, and make one criminal arrest per shift (Stamper 2005). The general philosophy of the San Diego administration was that an officer who was held to quantifiable statistics would have to be active in fighting crime.

Our interactions with patrol officers supported that philosophy. It is important to reemphasize that our argument, and this book, is not meant or to be understood as an attack on individual police officers as racists or bigots. While many of our vignettes portray situations involving individual police officers, these vignettes are used to underscore a much larger point: police officers perform in a fashion that is supported by their respective administrations and society at large. If police officers were not rewarded formally or informally for their productivity (number of contacts, citations, and arrests), then this book would likely be unnecessary, because officers would not proactively hunt in poor and minority neighborhoods. As will be discussed throughout this book, research has consistently supported what is anecdotally understood: that poor and racial minorities, and especially poor, racial minorities, are often the target of the police (for additional discussion see: Alpert, Dunham, and Smith 2007; Engel and Calnon 2004; Fagan, et al. 2009; Geller and Fagan 2010; Golub, Johnson, and Dunlap 2007; Eitle and Monahan 2009; Eitle, Stolzenberg, and D'Alessio 2005; Kane, Gustafson, and Bruell 2011; Reitzel, Rice, and Piquero 2004; Weitzer and Tuch 2004; and Zhao et al. 2011).

The evidence shows that when officers are expected to make a high number of citizen contacts, the discretionary decisions they make regarding who they should contact is influenced by society's views of who is criminal and who is not. Officers are shaped, as we all are, by the norms, cultural practices, and assumptions that have shaped the United States. There is a historical legacy of racism in the United States, and time has not eliminated this racial strife.[3]

Inherent Problems with Discretionary Proactivity

The choices police officers make regarding whether they will hunt, to what degree they will hunt, and what particular crimes they will hunt, largely influence how officers interact with the poorer members of a community. The question that needs to be asked, then, is "do we need patrol officers to be engaging in discretionary proactive missions?" In proactive cases, no citizen has requested the police work or asked the officer to correct a problem. No call has been made to the police department regarding criminal activity. Why, then, should officers be searching for suspected criminals whom they, themselves, identify? Such questions go to the heart of the role of the police in America. Allowing officers to, of their own volition, identify suspicious people and would-be criminals, gives the police an enormous amount of power. Unchecked discretion makes it extremely difficult to police the police. On the other hand, when a citizen asks for police assistance, the community is assured that police officers are not acting on their own beliefs about criminals, but rather are acting on the complaints of victims or witnesses.[4]

Democratic control over the police force is severely undermined when officers have wide discretion regarding what they do with their time when not responding to citizen calls for service. Perhaps, in theory, the proposition that officers should pursue people whom they believe may be engaging in criminal activity, basing that pursuit on their professional experience, is not objectionable, but this book illuminates the repercussions of such discretionary actions.

Criminal behavior is defined by what police identify as criminal. Police actions that the police label as criminal (see Jacob 1973) are mediated by what the legislature defines as such through the penal code, but the penal code, and the vehicle code especially, is so expansive that it allows officers almost unlimited discretion. Proactivity in conjunction with discretion is an additional way that officers identify potential criminals. To use the words of the officers, they identify economically poor people through focusing on "dirtbag" cars and label the occupants as likely deviants or "scumbags." This proactive behavior often negatively affects relationships between the police and poor communities.

We are strictly concerned here with issues of street crimes such as drug sales, illegal drug use, possession of drug paraphernalia, and prostitution because they are the target of patrol officer proactivity. These crimes are also largely considered victimless crimes. For example, when a drug arrest is made, an officer identifies the state (for example, New York) as the victim. Victimless, or street crimes, are also often the infractions that are targeted by criminal justice professionals and politicians to illustrate a "tough on crime" approach.

While we argue against patrol officers' investigation into what they, themselves, deem suspicious activities, we do not mean to suggest that investigation is always suspect. On the contrary, when citizens identify wrongdoing or claim to be victims of a crime, officers have an obligation to investigate. The key variable in our argument is who claims a wrong: a citizen or an officer?

Consequences of Discretionary Proactive Policing

Beginning in the 1970s, social scientists began to ask why racial disparities existed in the criminal justice system. Examinations into possible racism or bias within the criminal justice system resulted in a variety of findings. Some researchers found that the degree of punishment racial minorities receive is influenced by the race of the victim, the type of crime, and the region of the country in which the crime occurred (Free 2002; Hawkins 1987; Hymes et al. 2001; Walker, Spohn, and DeLone 1996, 2000; Weidner, Frase, and Schultz 2005). Overall, Black citizens are arrested in higher proportion to their population than Whites, with the disparity rising as the seriousness of the crime increases (LaFree 1995). Research has also found arrest warrants for Whites are more often denied by the district attorney's office, meaning the police are willing to arrest non-Whites on weaker evidence than they are Whites (Hepburn 1978).

Recently, the NYPD's active stop-and-frisk program revealed the following: (1) the number of stop-and-frisks had increased from 97,000 in 2002 to almost 700,000 in 2011; (2) only about 6 percent of the stops led to arrests; (3) in thirty-three precincts, Blacks and Latinos accounted for more than 90 percent of the stop-and-frisks; (4) in the six out of ten precincts with the lowest Black and Latino populations, these groups accounted for more than 70 percent of the stop-and-frisks; and (5) young Black and Latino men aged 14–24 accounted for 42 percent of all stop-and-frisks, yet they only represented 5 percent of the city's population (New York Civil Liberties Union 2012). Taken together, these study results lead to further questions regarding why police officers stop Black and Latino drivers and pedestrians in higher proportions.

A knee-jerk response by some is to reduce such behavior to simple racism, but our observations lead us to believe the situation is much more complicated. Specifically, the reasons for these disparities are related to institutional incentives and the policing subculture, which induce officers to engage in crime-fighting behavior that leads to proactive police activity. The need for officers to illustrate that they are "doing something"—fighting crime—leads to discretionary proactive behavior.[5] This insidious "doing something" is supported by police administrations and the stereotype of a "real" police officer, but it has crippling effects on disadvantaged communities.

Our research demonstrates that officers' decisions to simply stop and contact a citizen regardless of an arrest situation can have serious consequences for residents; these decisions are, therefore, important to study. In our research, only twelve arrests were made in over 300 hours of observation. Conley (2002) argued that the only way to understand arrest decisions is through observation of police in the field.[6] Our study uses field observation and interviews and contributes to the body of literature by detailing what influences the actions of officers when dealing with diverse communities. Furthermore, we discuss how persons who enter the criminal justice system, who are disproportionally non-White, are more likely to stay trapped in the system because of how police officers use the status of probation or parole as a tool for meeting their crime-fighting goals (Chapter 5). That activity in particular is illustrative of the larger phenomenon of the criminal justice system's orientation toward continued levels of surveillance of people who are deemed socially undesirable.

CHAPTER TWO

SETTING THE STAGE

Stonesville and Seaside

We do things different around here.

— Seaside officer

n this chapter we describe how our study was conducted and provide relevant contextual information for the following chapters.[1] The primary data sources for this research are observations and interviews with "Stonesville" and "Seaside" police officers. We do not to use the names of the actual cities nor identify by real name any of the officers observed or interviewed. *Stonesville* is a pseudonym for a medium-sized city in California and *Seaside* is a pseudonym for a large East Coast city in an unnamed state.[2] The Stonesville interviews and observations were conducted from the beginning of July through November 2000 (with one in-depth interview and ride-along in June of 2001) resulting in 25 in-depth interviews and 147 observational periods or ride-alongs.[3] In Seaside the interviews and observations were completed between late May and August 2010, based on 163 ride-alongs. Not only does the research benefit from including very different cities, but it also allows for an analysis both pre- and post-September 11, 2001. While all locales differ to some degree, there is no indication that these cities are outliers in terms of how criminal justice professionals make discretionary decisions. Their economic conditions at the time of each period of research are also typical to other similarly sized cities.

During the combined ride-alongs in both cities, we observed 310 police mobilizations, which included both dispatches to citizen calls for service and proactive contacts. The shortest period observed was a little under two hours, but sometimes we interacted with officers for an entire ten-hour shift. The average amount of time spent with each officer was almost six hours, for a combined total of over 310 hours of observation. There were differences between the two sites regarding how long the officers let us ride with them. In Stonesville, officers were more generous with their time. But even with less time spent observing, we saw more mobilizations in Seaside than in Stonesville, which is likely because of the differences in the cities' sizes and demand for police services.

While the data was collected ten years apart, little had changed in those ten years in the Stonesville Police Department. The Department's policing strategies and the ways it deploys officers are the same. The city's demographics also have changed only minimally. The true test, however, of the relevance of the 2000 Stonesville data is the degree to which it is comparable to the 2010 Seaside data. In almost all respects, we observed the same behaviors in Seaside as we had in Stonesville. Officers interviewed in Seaside in 2010 had similar comments and opinions about proactive policing as officers in Stonesville in 2000. Chapters 3 and 4 clearly illustrate that discretionary proactive policing was the same across the decade and on the two coasts.

Although we officially rode with fifty officers (twenty-five in Stonesville and twenty-five in Seaside), we observed many additional officers at different mobilizations. For each police mobilization, the number of officers on the scene and often the names of the additional officers were recorded. Between citizen calls and proactive activities, and because most police mobilizations

Table 2.1. General Characteristics of Police Mobilizations and
Police Officers in Stonesville and Seaside

	Stonesville	Seaside
Number of police mobilizations observed	147	163
Number of reactive police mobilizations	117	115
Number of proactive police mobilizations	30	48
Average time of ride-along	7+ hours	5+ hours
Total observation time	201 hours	111 hours
Number of officers observed	25	25
Average years of officer experience	3+ years	7+ years
Average officer age	30.6	31.4

included more than one officer, a total of 279 different officers were
observed. Overall, over 600 different citizen-officer interactions
were witnessed.

The fifty officers who were observed and interviewed varied in
many important ways. The ethnicity of the fifty officers roughly estimated the diversity of both patrol forces. Sixteen percent of ride-
alongs were with female officers and 32 percent were with minority
officers (14 percent Black, 10 percent Latino, and 8 percent Asian).
Overall, our impression was that interviewees roughly represented
the force, however, representational deficiencies were somewhat
addressed in the opportunity to observe and interact with 279
different officers. Hence, while only nine Black officers were interviewed in depth, we observed and talked at varying lengths to
many other Black officers. The officers observed varied in years of
service on the force from twenty-nine years to one year, with an
average of 5.6 years. Overall, the Stonesville patrol force averaged
less than four years of service, compared to Seaside, where officers

averaged over seven years of service. The average age of the officers observed was 31 years (30.6 in Stonesville and 31.4 in Seaside). Both departments overwhelmingly deployed one-person police cars, and most of the ride-alongs were with only one officer. In Seaside, we rode with the districts' "6 squads," which led to observations where two and three officers were in the same car. These 6 squad units had more than one officer in the vehicle because they were specifically tasked with proactive work and were released from answering calls for service in order to give them the time to hunt. Initially, we planned to completely replicate the Stonesville study, but we quickly discovered that would be impossible since proactive work was largely practiced by these special 6 squad units in Seaside. So, in Seaside we spent time with members of the 6 squads and with typical line-level officers (18 percent of our observations were members of the 6 squad).

The one-person-per-car policing strategy was an advantage in our research because the answers to our questions were unconstrained by a peer observing.[4] Some officers would talk about other officers, which, of course, they would not have done if those officers were present. Officers were often forthright in their comments to us, sometimes surprisingly so. Many of them appeared happy to have someone to talk to and someone interested in their everyday work.[5] Two-person cars also had advantages. We could observe officers' interactions with one another as they hunted. In several instances, one officer would explain to the other why a particular stop should be made.

While the officers seemed generally cooperative in interviews, and we were able to observe their decisions, some of which are crucial to understanding the exercise of police discretion, studies of this sort have limitations. Police officers are suspicious of outsiders and are often guarded in their responses to questions (see Paoline

2004). This reticence, no doubt, affected the degree to which some officers were forthcoming about their policing decisions.

Because this study is about police officers in two departments in a country with thousands of departments, it may legitimately raise questions of generalizability. This research has, as its strength, its depth, not its breadth. Conducting interviews and gathering observational data rather than solely relying on arrest rates or calls for service or some other quantitative indicator of police discretion proved fertile. Arrest data can tell the researcher the location of the arrest, the suspected offense, the race of the suspect, and the name of the officer, though often all of these variables are not available. Often studies that rely on arrest data do not tell the researchers if the officer was familiar with the suspect, if it was a repeat call for service, what the attitudes of the officer and the suspect were, or the nature of the interaction. All of these factors are extremely important when attempting to understand police behavior and use of discretion. Besides the use of force, the decision to arrest is often the most important decision an officer makes. The choice to take away someone's freedom is an extremely serious one and is, therefore, a key decision to study. And yet, officers make many choices prior to an arrest, choices that greatly help explain the arrest decision and may not have been reflected in quantitative data. For example, officers make choices regarding where to patrol, which car to stop, and what questions to ask the citizens they contact. These preliminary choices, we argue, are paramount to understanding who enters the criminal justice system through arrest and why.

Americans have become increasingly interested in why officers choose to stop a vehicle or pedestrian. Particularly, there is fairly widespread concern regarding racial profiling by police officers. In order to identify how serious this problem is, many departments (and in some cases state highway patrols) have begun gathering data on vehicle stops. Stonesville is one city that chose to voluntarily administer such a study more than once. The initial study required officers to complete a form for each vehicle stop. The form included the reason the driver was stopped, the race and age of the driver, the action taken, the date and time of the stop, and the officer's badge number. Our observational period overlapped with the gathering of this data and, therefore, the observer was able to talk with the officers about it, and evaluate their behavior regarding it.

The profiling study provides a good example of the disadvantages of quantitative studies and the advantages of the observational data and interviews we gathered. Only one officer told us that he did not really "mind" the racial profiling study (he was a Latino officer). Every other officer we spoke with resented the study. In some cases officers asked us our opinions about the racial profiling study. Our answers influenced how cooperative they would be through the rest of the observation and interview period. When they were asked—"What do you think of this racial profiling study?"— officers responded that they felt they were being called racists, that the data would be held against them because they had to divulge their badge numbers, and that the study would not consider what type of district they patrolled (meaning if their district had a high proportion of minorities).[6]

As previously stated, every officer (with the one exception) said that he or she changed his or her behavior because of the racial profiling study. Not only did they share this change of behavior with us, but we observed it as well. What is interesting is that they did not all change their behavior in the same way. Many officers said the study had resulted in a reduction of vehicle stops, which was evident from radio traffic. In essence, officers were worried that traffic stops would now get them in trouble, and they felt that the stops created too much additional paperwork. Some other examples of changes in behavior included: only giving tickets to

White people, giving tickets to everyone they stopped instead of issuing some warnings as they previously had, and making fewer stops. In fact, one veteran officer (who could probably get away with it because of his seniority on the force) relayed that he was not going to make a single stop for the entire year. During our observation, a car dangerously sped through a red light, and the officer said, "Oh, well. I'm not stopping anybody." Another veteran officer we observed made numerous stops in a shift but did not fill out the survey for any of them.

The validity of the racial profiling study administered in Stonesville was completely undermined by the change in behavior of the officers. The researchers who conducted the racial profiling study had limited means to know about the altered policing strategies, because they did not systematically interview or observe officers.[7] The pitfalls of the methods used for the racial profiling study illustrate how observation of both police behavior and the choices they make is a valuable asset to the understanding of police discretion.

Stonesville

As of the 2000 census (relevant at the time of data gathering), Stones County, the county in which Stonesville resides, had a population of 1.2 million. The city itself encompasses 98 square miles with a population of approximately 400,000. Stonesville was fairly ethnically diverse; of the city population, 16 percent was Black, 21 percent Latino, 17 percent Asian or Pacific Islander, and the remaining approximately 48 percent White.[8] The number of county residents living below the poverty line fell at 13.7 percent of the total population. The size of these minority populations makes Stonesville a good site for studying officers' discretionary decisions given the concerns regarding the influence of a person's race on an officer's behavior (Table 2.2).

Like other cities, in the late 1990s and early 2000s, Stonesville

Table 2.2. City and Police Department Characteristics

	Stonesville	Seaside
City population	400,000 (2000)	900,000+ (2010)
Percent non-White residents	52 (2000)	60 (2010)
Percent residents living at or below the poverty line	13.7 (2000)	25 (2010)
Sworn police personnel	664	6,800+
Line officers	242	3,900+
Approximate number of calls for service	750,000 (1998)	1,800,000 (2010)
Internal Affairs investigations	79 (1998)	781 (2010)

experienced a decline in Uniform Crime Report (UCR) offenses, with the exception of rape. The two offenses which fell considerably below the national average of all cities in 1999 (the year which immediately preceded this research) were murder (−26 percent) and robbery (−25 percent). Criminal activity in Stonesville, then, was fairly typical for a city of its size.

THE STONESVILLE POLICE DEPARTMENT

When the research for this study was completed, the total number of sworn police officers in Stonesville was 664. Of those officers, 526 served at the line level, leaving 136 in leadership positions. There were approximately 242 officers assigned to patrol (including trainees who were on the street); they are the focus of this study. Approximately 19 percent of the police department staff were women. The ethnic breakdown of the police department roughly reflected the Stonesville city population: 8 percent of the staff were Black, 12 percent Latino, 8 percent Asian, 1 percent American Indian, and 2 percent Filipino. Communities in recent years have asked their police departments to "look" more like the community they patrol. Stonesville would seem to have fulfilled that request.

A closer examination of the positions minorities and women held within the department reflected that most of the diversity was found within the civilian component of the staff. For example, only 16 percent of the line officers policing the streets of Stonesville were women. Black officers constituted 6 percent of the staff at the officer level. Of the line level officers, 11 percent were Latino, 15 percent Asian, 1 percent American Indian, and 3 percent Filipino. Asians were clearly the best-represented minority.

According to the Bureau of Justice Statistics, in 2000, 29 percent of officers in departments with 100 or more officers were minorities (Reaves and Hickman 2000). When the number of Blacks, Latinos, and Asians were combined for the Stonesville police force, it consisted of 33 percent minorities, which was well above the national average. At the time this research was conducted, the Stonesville's police chief was a minority, and officers attributed his recruiting policies to the increased diversity of the force. We rarely encountered a veteran minority officer, which seems to support the idea that the greater representation of minorities was a fairly recent development. Other research has also found that minority chiefs are more likely to employ a diverse police force (Zhao, He, and Lovrich 2005).

Citizen complaints against Stonesville police officers had not been inordinately high. For example, in 1998 there were seventy-nine internal affairs investigations, including four investigations into use of excessive force. There were a combined total of forty-one investigations in the areas of dishonesty, conduct unbecoming, harassment, and discourtesy. There were eight investigations into allegations of improper searches or tactics. These numbers may seem shockingly low considering the patrol division handles approximately 750,000 calls for service in a year; however, such rates are not uncommon, given that, nationally, police departments sustain an average of only 10 percent of citizen complaints reviewed internally (Pate and Fridell 1993).[9]

Also, as was common in police departments nationwide, Stonesville was divided into geographic patrol areas. The four patrol sectors were North, Central, East, and South, with each sector divided into seven to nine patrol districts for a total of twenty-nine districts. Reportedly, the average number of calls for service a district received determined the number of patrol cars assigned to that district. A captain managed each patrol sector and supervised three watch commanders (lieutenants), an executive lieutenant, and eight sergeants.

The patrol schedule consisted of three ten-hour shifts, with the busier times of the day having a slight overlap between shifts. The day shift began at 6:00 A.M. and ended at 4:00 P.M. The swing shift, which had the greatest number of officers, started at 3:00 P.M. and ended at 1:00 A.M. The third major shift of the day was graveyard, which began at 9:00 P.M. and ended at 7:00 A.M. Officers could take a 45-minute lunch when calls for service were infrequent. They had no other scheduled breaks, but they took them as needed or as they were able. Because the officers worked ten-hour days, they had a four-day workweek.

Stonesville Police Department's leadership was committed to the community-oriented policing philosophy. Two stations provided a base for all four of the patrol sectors. The North Station was the base for patrol officers in the North and Central sectors and the South Station provided a base for service to the South and East sectors. The department created a decentralized model to allow for closer and more frequent interaction between police officers and the community.

The two stations created an interesting dynamic among the patrol staff. There was some degree of animosity between the North and South stations. While the two stations divided the police force so they were in more locations in the community, they also divided the staff symbolically. Officers repeatedly asked us to compare the two stations and the officers based at each. The North station officers told us they felt the South station was micromanaged and had to deal with citizens who were always complaining about their rights. On the other hand, South station officers complained that the North station officers were, in one officer's words, "hard chargers." Simply stated, North station officers had the reputation of searching for crime and putting other patrol duties as lower priorities. For example, they may have decided to stop an automobile they believed looked suspicious before they responded to a citizen call sent out by dispatch.

Cultural Differences in Stonesville Stations

We'll see in Chapter 4 that differences in the two stations affect levels of officers' productivity. Here, we explain those variances in order to provide necessary context. North station officers were considered the more traditional "tough guy" cops and South station officers were often described as more professionalized (although not favorably). Observations revealed some truth to these characterizations. South station officers were often concerned about the law and how it pertained to their specific actions. For example, they would discuss among themselves what constituted a consent search and what could be included in that search. They also discussed what gave them probable cause to arrest an individual and what did not, however, in all the hours with the North station, we only heard someone discuss law once, and it was in the following manner: "The Supreme Court says that as a ride-a-long you can't go into houses without the permission of the owner. But that doesn't hold out here. These people don't know and don't care. So you just go wherever I go."

Another example of the differing levels of professionalism between the two stations was found in roll call. Roll call is a meeting run by the sergeants who start off every shift. The purpose of these meetings is to relay information to the patrol officers. Any updates on "wanted" people or department functions are given, the sergeant assigns each officer to a district, and a video is sometimes shown. Videos are often made by the media department of the force so that the same information can get to the over 500 line officers; the videos often include segments on upcoming department events and information that could be considered in-service training. For example, during our observations videos included information on gang activity in the area, how to treat drunk-in-public offenders, and how to cite scooter violations.

During roll calls in the North area the sergeants would make some announcements about suspects or recent arrests that were especially noteworthy. They would then ask if anyone had anything to add. It was extremely rare that anyone had anything to add, and when someone did say something, it was relatively superficial, like commenting on the quality of the pursuit the previous evening. Then a video might have been played. Afterwards they were dismissed. The entirety of roll call typically lasted ten minutes.

The atmosphere in the North station during roll call was slightly rambunctious and resistant. Patrol officers clearly felt as if it was an unimportant part of their job and that they should be out on the streets, instead. There was a lot of camaraderie that occurred before (sometimes during) and after roll call.[10] For example, one would ask another if anything exciting had happened on his days off or if he ended up "booking" someone from a call the previous evening. Officers almost always talked over the playing of the video and paid little attention to it. Sometimes there were comments made ridiculing those staff members who took part in the production of the video, as well. Roll call was generally treated as an irrelevant nuisance that the officers had to endure, but that they ignored.

Roll call in the South station had a completely different feel; the officers seemed to generally have a different attitude. Officers discussed information they had learned at conferences and from books or magazines. They watched the entire video without talking during it. When asked if they had anything to contribute, officers often told the group about a development that occurred earlier in the week or mentioned something they had recently learned. South station officers also asked many more questions of the sergeants, as if information was an ally. Following the general meeting, the sub-areas (South and East) would meet separately with their respective sergeants to discuss any problems or issues. The North and Central sectors in the North station rarely had such meetings; the only time we observed them at the North station was during a couple of graveyard shifts, and these meetings were small and conducted more quickly. Overall, from the behavior and atmosphere during roll calls, observing officers from the different areas on patrol, and listening to them speak about themselves and officers from the other section, the stations appeared to have distinctive organizational cultures that affected their level of professionalism.

The management and the organizational culture of each of the stations seemed to maintain these characteristics among the officers, but officers also had some choice in where they patrolled, which worked to perpetuate these differences in professionalism. As mentioned, the organizational culture of each station was both understood and discussed by officers and influenced their choices of sectors and shifts. Once a year, officers requested days of the week, sectors, and shifts they wanted to work. Those with the most seniority chose first, which usually resulted in the most veteran officers working days during the week and the most junior officers working graveyards on the weekends. There were some veterans who enjoyed working graveyard shifts, but for the most part the pattern held true. This selection process also resulted in dividing the workforce so that those who fit the culture of the South station signed-up for either the South or East sectors, and those who preferred the culture of the North station requested either the North or Central sectors.

Sergeants also affected the choices of officers. There were particular sergeants who were considered incompetent or disagreeable, and they were avoided. Unfortunately, that usually meant the sergeants with the least respect (perhaps in some cases rightly so) were assigned the most junior officers who could not get on any other team. Teams were groups of people who worked the same days, shifts, and sectors. For each shift there were two teams, the junior and the senior team. There was some overlap, but generally the senior team had the better days off—for instance, Saturdays, Sundays, and Mondays. Each sergeant worked with a specific team. For example, one sergeant might have worked with the day shift on Tuesdays through Fridays in the East sector. While the administration tried to ensure that all teams had some senior members, there was a noticeable difference in years of experience when comparing teams.

Seaside

Seaside is much larger than Stonesville. According to the 2010 Census, the population in that year was greater than 900,000 people. Seaside was also much more ethnically diverse. Whites and Blacks were both around 40 percent of the city population, with the percentage being a little bit higher for Blacks. About 12 percent of the population was Latino. Slightly over 25 percent of the city lived at or below the poverty line. There were neighborhoods of concentrated wealth, as well as apartment buildings and housing developments that were maintained by the city's housing development agency (see Table 2.2).

In 2010, similar to most cities in the United States, Seaside experienced a decrease in UCR offenses, however, the violent crime reduction in Seaside was not as sharp as in other larger U.S. cities. Seaside saw a 3 percent reduction in violent crime, compared to the 6 percent decline nationwide. Overall, though, Seaside's crime rate was typical of most large American cities.

Seaside was a much more crime-ridden city than Stonesville. Shootings occurred daily. The higher crime environment was reflected in our observations. In one case there was an armed home invasion and in another a shooting in which bullets went right through a car with children in it. Officers also found themselves at higher risk of being victimized by violence. One officer we observed was shot at just minutes after our observer had departed. We were required to wear bulletproof vests in Seaside ride-alongs; in Stonesville the issue of a vest was not even mentioned.

THE SEASIDE POLICE DEPARTMENT

The Seaside Police Department was a much larger agency, having almost 7,000 sworn officers compared to fewer than 700 in Stonesville. The sheer size of a department, of course, leads to all kinds of additional characteristics. In Seaside, there were many more ranks and special divisions than in Stonesville. Almost 3,000 of Seaside's officers were assigned to over 90 special units, leaving about 4,000 officers delegated for regular patrol. Civilians worked in only 20 percent of the department's positions, although the national average of civilians in a department was 46 percent (UCR 2008).

While many departments had by this time moved to hiring civilians in more positions in police departments as a component of community policing, that had not happened in Seaside. Routine data entry positions were even staffed by sworn officers. Patrol officers sang the praises of Seaside's system, because if they were hurt, they knew they would be reassigned to one of the desk jobs inside the district offices. Some also appreciated the ability to spend short periods of time "inside" if they wanted a break from the streets.

For the size of the Seaside Police Department and the number of calls for service it received, there were relatively few citizen complaints against its officers. In 2010, there were 781 internal affairs investigations, including 301 into allegations of excessive force, with 182 exonerations and withdrawn or unfounded claims. Although there were a significant number of investigations for both misconduct (223) and verbal abuse (151), in each of these areas over half of the complaints were unsustained (65 percent for each classification). There were over 100 investigations into other matters.

The city is divided into six sectors with three or four districts in each and hundreds of officers for each sector. When we observed them, 40 percent of the officers served in special teams, leaving the other 60 percent in the regular patrol division. Most of the special teams were proactive units that did not answer calls for service. Occasionally these special teams did monitor the radio and chose to respond to a scene. For example, on one observed ride-along, when an officer was dispatched to a residence where the callers were afraid that a man was about to molest a little girl, a special team which was monitoring the radio also responded immediately.

In reality, the number of special units, or proactive teams, was larger than 90 because each district had its own 6 squad or "captain's squad." The officers who made up those squads were handpicked by the captains. The assignment was considered recognition of being a "good cop" and "hard worker." If officers wanted to be members of a 6 squad, they needed to do something to distinguish themselves from other officers. One officer who was hoping to be on the 6 squad said he was very happy that he had recently made a high profile arrest because he thought it would help his chances of being selected by his captain for the 6 squad. When asked what he thought he would need to do to be reassigned, he reported that it was clear to him that he had to make a lot of contacts and be regularly engaged in proactive work, including vehicle and pedestrian stops. One officer who had been a member of the 6 squad lamented that she was put back on regular patrol. She said the reason was because she did not do enough proactive work. Her preference, she said, was to respond to calls for service, and she thought that made her a good team player.

The 6 squads were the most visual proactive units for line officers, because line officers interacted with 6 squad members in their district office they could see them in their own districts. Other proactive units worked city-wide or at the sector level rather than the district level. The officers in the 6 squads, like other proactive teams, were dispatched to calls for service only in the most affluent and lowest crime district in the city. The 6 squads were also the first step to joining more elite proactive city-wide units, such as the Strike Forces, Narcotics units, or SWAT. Officers were not assigned to special city-wide units until they had proven their worth in a 6 squad.

The result of having so many proactive teams — 40 percent of officers were assigned to them — was that "regular" patrol officers were given the message that their main responsibility was to answer calls for service so that the other units could do the "real police work." As compared to Stonesville, this resulted in fewer proactive contacts for patrol officers, especially if an officer was not interested in being assigned to a special team.

The 6 squads and other proactive units are important to our story. They are clear illustrations of how organizational incentives are created that result in officers either doing discretionary proactive work or not. "Hey, proactive work is *their* job" was an attitude that seemed prevalent. If the patrol officers did not want to become "one of them," then they engaged in little discretionary proactive patrol.

At times, Seaside utilized COMPSTAT activities. In those cases, proactive units were assigned to focus on a specific geographic area and/or criminal offense. Teams would be assigned to a particular area for a weekend and a high volume of officers would saturate the area (for example, groups of fifteen officers would walk the streets together), sometimes in the company of other community criminal justice professionals such as probation or patrol units.

In general, the 6 squad officers engaged in similar proactive policing strategies as Stonesville officers. Their captain might tell them to focus on a particular offense that week (in one district it was curfews), but largely they were just expected to make citizen contacts, so their proactive work was highly discretionary. Like we found in Stonesville, the officers in Seaside chose where, who, and what was done largely by patrolling the district until they found a vehicle or pedestrian who appeared to be suspicious. How that process looked is detailed in Chapters 3 and 4.

One way in which district administration kept track of both proactive and reactive contacts was that each officer had to complete an activity log. Each call for service answered, ticket written, pedestrian or vehicle stop made was supposed to be documented in the officer's activity log. Some officers were more diligent about filling out the forms than others. Officers who were on the 6 squads were sure to record their contacts, because they knew that was what they needed to do in order to stay on the 6 squad. Officers who were hoping to become a member of a 6 squad were also very sure to record everything they did; their diligence might help them stand out to their superiors.

The relationships between 6 squad members and "regular" patrol officers varied, but in most districts they appeared to be tense or unpleasant. Patrol officers would tell us that 6 squad officers could go home early or were treated better by the captain. Some mentioned that they did not think the 6 squad was "all that great," even though it was supposed to be filled with the best officers. There was an expressed feeling that 6 squad officers were the captain's favorites, and when captains changed, so would the 6 squad officers. Based on a couple of relayed stories, our observations confirmed that in some cases, 6 squad membership did change when a new captain came to the district.

Seaside officers did not get to choose their districts but, instead, were assigned to them. The only exception to this was when an officer was shot; then she was allowed to select her district upon her return, and was envied by other officers as a result. From our observations, it appeared that the administration assigned officers to districts that reflected those officers demographically. For example, if a district was heavily populated with Black people, then Black officers would make up most of the ranks of that district. This was especially true in districts where there might have been a language barrier between the officers and the residents. For example, there was a sizable community of people of Puerto Rican descent in a certain district, and most of the officers who worked there spoke Spanish.

Police Mobilizations

Of the 310 police mobilizations[11] observed in Seaside and Stonesville, 75 percent were reactive situations, which are qualitatively different from proactive situations in that they do not require the officers to spend any time initiating the interaction. In reactive situations, officers are told to respond to an incident, and they do so directly (although, admittedly, at different speeds depending on the severity of emergency). Alternatively, in proactive situations officers spend, on average, thirty to forty-five minutes hunting for that "great stop."

The vast majority of observed police mobilizations did not involve a crime; this supports the findings of other researchers who have concluded that patrol officers do not spend most of their time fighting crime (Famega 2005; Greene 1989; Bittner 1990; Goldstein 1979; Wilson 1968). As an example, according to the 2010 Uniform Crime Reports there were over 13 million arrests in the United States — excluding traffic violations — and of these arrests only 522,077 were for a violent crime, a rate of 4 percent. Between the Seaside and Stonesville, only 11 percent of observed police mobilizations (both reactive and proactive) were defined by officers as incidents in which someone had committed a crime. Almost 90 percent of observed police mobilizations resulted in police concluding that no crime had occurred.[12] For an incident or citizen call for service to be considered a crime by a police officer, according to observations and interviews of officers, two conditions must be present. First, a suspect or persuasive complainant must be at the scene. Second, the responding officer(s) must deem the act criminal. Hence, a crime may have actually occurred, but if officers find no evidence of a crime when they respond to the location of the citizen call, then no crime is recorded in any manner. For the most part, if officers do not find any witness to explain what happened, they have no evidence to conclude a crime has occurred.[13] Most mobilizations did not deal with legal issues at all. In both cities combined, slightly over 70 percent of observed police mobilizations revealed that no infraction of any kind had occurred, meaning that not even a moving violation was at issue. In Stonesville, 8 percent, and in Seaside, 5 percent of observations included officers issuing someone a traffic ticket. In general, traffic stops were less frequent among the line patrol officers in Seaside when compared to Stonesville because, as will be discussed in Chapters 3 and 4, Seaside officers were more likely to make pedestrian stops. Overall, another 6 percent of police mobilizations involved an incident where someone had committed a vehicle infraction and the officer(s) chose to warn the driver rather than issue a ticket

Table 2.3. Specific Details about Police Mobilizations

	Stonesville (%)	Seaside (%)
Proactive police mobilizations	21	29
Police mobilizations where no crime was committed	90	87
Police mobilizations where some type of crime was committed	10	13
Police mobilizations where a traffic ticket was issued	8	5

(warning the driver without issuing a citation only happened once in Seaside).

Perhaps because officers know that citizen calls are unlikely to be criminal in nature, they are unlikely to proceed to dispatched calls quickly. The average of the two cities saw 72 percent of police mobilizations in which officers responded in a routine fashion, meaning the officer obeyed all traffic laws and regulations. There was quite a difference between the cities, though, in how frequently they responded routinely: in Stonesville 80 percent and in Seaside 64 percent. This is likely because of Seaside's higher crime rate, which would understandably result in a quicker response from law enforcement. Overall, 16 percent of the time officers responded to a dispatch in an urgent manner. In a small percentage of instances (8 percent), officers viewed the dispatch as so unimportant that they did other things on the way to the location of the citizen call. For example, officers would stop and talk with peers or people on the street, or stop to get something to drink.

When officers approached citizens, they largely did so in a composed manner, using normal conversation tones without threatening language or displaying any type of weapon. Over 94 percent of observed police mobilizations in both cities resulted in the com-

posed approach of the officer or officers involved. Officers sometimes became agitated during a citizen interaction, but they largely
began the contact in a professional, collected way. Situations where
officers were most likely to become visibly agitated included those
incidents in which claims of bias were made. Numerous officers
— both White and non-White — lost their composure when they
were accused of being racist in some way, a situation which is discussed in more detail later in this chapter.

In many instances, officers did not interact with victims or complainants. Our observations found a combined 59 percent of police
mobilizations did not involve any interaction with a victim or complainant (76 percent for Seaside and 40 percent for Stonesville).
This percentage is high for a variety of reasons. Some calls for service occurred when an afterhours burglary alarm had been acti-
vated. When officers responded to the building to see if a burglary
had occurred, they very rarely encountered anyone at the scene. In
other cases, citizens called in the address or street where a noise
problem was occurring, but they themselves did not wish to be
contacted. In Seaside, officers would respond to noise or disorder
complaints only to find neither problems nor people at the scene
when they arrived. Sometimes neighbors would call because they
thought violence was occurring next door, but when the police arrived there was no evidence of any assault. There were also some
instances where both the victim and suspect had fled the scene.
In proactive contacts, of course, because there was no victim with
whom to interact, there were many different types of police mobilizations that resulted in no contact with complainants or victims.

In none of our observations did an officer ask a citizen to sign
a misdemeanor complaint. Brown (1981) explained that officers
will ask citizens to make a complaint when they believe the situation merits an arrest because of its seriousness or their inability
to resolve it in a more satisfactory manner (see also Mastrofski

et al. 2000). When individuals want to make a citizen's arrest, it creates more work for officers, both in terms of paperwork and time at the scene. In one shoplifting incident, an officer told a store clerk that he could not arrest the suspect (unless the clerk had the theft on videotape) because the clerk had not seen the incident. The clerk began looking through the tape and continued to insist that "something happen" to the accused thief. The officer repeatedly tried to dissuade the clerk from filing a complaint by telling her she would have to appear in court, or she could be sued for false imprisonment. There were only two observations (both in Stonesville) where complainants or victims really insisted on wanting to "press charges."

Police-citizen contact over a typical officer's shift was sporadic. Overall, we observed a little more than one citizen-police interaction per hour—1.28 (0.80 per hour in Stonesville with a high of 1.67 per hour and 1.71 in Seaside with a high of 4.67).[14] Time on the scene of a reactive call ranged from less than one minute (when no one was at the scene) to over one hour. The complexity of the incident and the level of mediation needed influenced the time spent on the scene. Furthermore, if an arrest was required, the length of the interaction was at least doubled. One observed Stonesville arrest took over an hour and a half in the jail alone because there were so many arrestees to be processed by the sheriff's deputies. In Seaside, arresting officers who had to take their detainee to the Department's central facility were devoted to that case for at least a couple of hours.

Police mobilizations largely took place in lower income and commercial areas. In both cities, about 50 percent of observed police mobilizations occurred in lower income neighborhoods. Commercial areas saw the second largest number of police mobilizations, at 24 percent in Stonesville and 21 percent in Seaside. These were largely the result of tripped burglar alarms and robbery calls.

There were, however, exceptions. For example, a 6 squad in Seaside that worked in a very affluent neighborhood made a bicycle stop of a young man in a commercial parking lot. That unit specifically complained about the lack of opportunity to do proactive work, given the district they were assigned. Middle class neighborhoods only saw 20 percent of the observed police mobilizations in Stonesville and only 2 percent in Seaside. Given the demography of the two cities, this disparity is not too surprising. Seaside had many more poor neighborhoods and more officers in them. We only observed a combined total of three police mobilizations in an upper class neighborhood.

Not only did police mobilizations largely occur in lower class areas, they also most often involved suspects of color. Of the 121 identified suspects in observed police mobilization in Stonesville, 71 percent were non-White individuals compared to an overwhelming 81 percent of the 97 suspects in Seaside. Calls for service or reactive contacts and, especially, proactive contacts were overwhelmingly made between officers and non-White suspects. Suspects were people who either the police or complainants identified as possible lawbreakers. Seaside's suspects were largely either Puerto Rican or Black. In Stonesville, 47 percent of identified suspects were Black. This percentage seems particularly high in Stonesville given only 16 percent of the population was Black (United States Census 2000). The percentage of Black suspects in Seaside (60 percent) was more in line with its proportion of Black residents (40 percent), but there was still a marked disproportion. An additional 21 percent of suspects in Stonesville and 19 percent in Seaside were Latino, and only 3 percent of suspects were Asian in Stonesville (Seaside did not have any Asian suspects). Whites were considered suspects in 28 percent of mobilizations in Stonesville and 19 percent in Seaside.

Table 2.4. Police Mobilizations by Neighborhood and Race
of the Suspect

	Stonesville (%)*	Seaside (%)*
Police mobilizations in lower income neighborhoods	51	53
Police mobilizations in middle income neighborhoods	20	2
Police mobilizations in upper income neighborhoods	0	1
Police mobilizations in commercial areas	24	21
Police mobilizations in other areas (parks, mixed use)	4	24
Identified suspects who were non-White	72	81
Identified suspects by race	47 (Black)* 28 (White) 21 (Latino) 3 (Asian)	60 (Black) 19 (Latino) 19 (White) 2 (Other)

* Rounding errors

When officers interacted with people during calls for service, they usually did so in pairs. In our observations, the median number of officers who responded per call for service was two in Stonesville, compared to three in Seaside.[15] This is partly explained by the fact that the 6 squads in Seaside almost always rode in teams of at least two per car. Several observations were of a team of three 6 squad members who all rode in the same car. In most reactive situations, two officers were assigned by dispatch to a particular situation. In some cases, the first officer to arrive on the scene may have radioed that he or she could handle the incident alone. There were also situations when the first officer to respond realized that there was no complainant at the scene and, for this reason, radioed that no other officers needed to respond. In Seaside, officers often called off their peers on "shots-fired" calls because there was no evidence of a firearm having been discharged when they arrived on the scene.

Proactive interactions that were *not* initiated by proactive units were more likely to have only one officer at the scene, especially at the beginning of the incident. The median number of officers in observed proactive contacts was 1 in Stonesville compared to 1.64 in Seaside (largely explained by the inclusion of 6 squad teams in Seaside).[16] In proactive observations when more than one officer was on the scene, additional officers arrived after the first officer had made the contact. For example, when officers made traffic stops, they reported over the radio their location and what car they were stopping. Reporting their location was important for safety purposes so that if anything were to happen to the officers, dispatch and the officers' colleagues would know their whereabouts. The other function of this announcement was so that other patrol officers in the area could back-up the officer on the scene. Like reactive situations, the number of officers present at the scene of an incident increased when the incident escalated in complexity and danger. One such observation occurred when a sergeant stopped a vehicle for crossing two lanes of a highway and then exiting on a one-way ramp going the wrong direction. The driver of the vehicle became increasingly belligerent during the traffic stop, and the sergeant consequently called for other officers to respond to the scene.[17] The number of officers on the scene was just one way proactive situations were qualitatively different from reactive situations. The following chapters will explain how these contacts were different in other ways, as well.

Conclusion

This chapter outlined some of the characteristics of Stonesville's and Seaside's police departments that are important for an understanding of the context of the officers' work. The difference in city size and area of the country is a strength of the study. The institutional incentives to proactively police were somewhat different, but were present in both cities. In Stonesville, the administrative and internal departmental pressure was more diffuse. Basically, the administration (and fellow officers) expected proactive work because that was the work of "good" cops, it was what the city wanted, and they thought it was important to be crime fighters. In Seaside, the incentives were much more direct—"good" cops were on the 6 squad. If you wanted to be on the 6 squad, you had to do proactive work. You had to make arrests. Your activity log each shift needed to be full. While the incentives to hunt were more obvious in Seaside, observations showed discretionary proactive policing was completed in the same manner in both cities with just a few exceptions, such as more focus on pedestrian stops in Seaside.

CHAPTER THREE

SHAKEN OR STIRRED?

Choosing Your Policing Style
and Level of Proactivity

Everyone in this district is on probation
or parole. They're all searchable.
— Stonesville officer

ith the advent of the 9-1-1 system, researchers concluded
that patrol officers continue to spend a greater proportion of their time responding to citizen calls for service
than proactively fighting crime (Black 1980; Garland 2001: Smith,
Novak, and Frank 2001). Dispatchers prioritize calls and send officers to respond based on the immediacy of need. Even in high-
crime districts, though, most nights leave a lot of time for an officer
to fill as she sees fit (Brown 1981). Studies have demonstrated that
approximately half (Bittner 1990, Reiss 1971) to three-quarters (Famega, Frank, and Mazerolle 2005) of an officer's shift is discretionary or "clear" time.

Police officers decide what type of officer they want to be before
stepping into the patrol car each day. Does an officer want to be
a "hard charger" who spends much of his unassigned time looking for lawbreakers? If so, is he interested in targeting stolen cars,
drugs, weapons, or people who are searchable because of their probation or parole status? Or, instead, does the officer want to mini-
mize his proactive activities and use his unassigned time to make

contacts with community members or wait in his patrol car until he is dispatched to a call for service? Answers to these questions all influence an officer's *policing style* and, therefore, his decisions on the street. This chapter highlights decisions officers make before they even start their shifts; the types of offenses they decide to hunt are important discretionary decisions that influence their policing styles. As it concerns proactivity, there are three different policing styles that emerged — hunters, slugs, and community builders. Our observations suggested that choice of policing style was influenced by a variety of factors, including an officer's number of years on the force, the sex of the officer, and, in the case of Stonesville, the officer's experiences during his training period and his sergeant's management approach. There were also institutional incentives and disincentives to proactive policing that affected officers' styles. An officer's policing style influenced her likelihood to arrest in a given situation. If she came across the crime she was hunting, she would be more likely to arrest in that case because her hunting efforts would have proved successful.

Police Discretion and Style

The discussion related to police officer discretion is wide and varied.[1] Social scientists have identified four factors as major influences on how police officers use their discretion. Perhaps most obviously, the characteristics of the crime affect the degree to which an officer can wield discretion. First, officers have much less freedom to ignore serious offenses. Second, the relationship between the suspect and the victim influences police discretion: the closer the victim-suspect relationship, the greater the use of discretion. Third, the relationship between the police officer and the subject or victim also affects how police officers use their discretion. Included in this relationship is the oft-cited influence of the suspect's attitude toward the officer (Black 1980; Engel, Sobol, and Worden

2000; Reisig et al. 2004 Worden and Shepard 1996).[2] Finally, police department administration's policies shape officer discretion to some degree (Groeneveld 2005; Skolnick 1966; Wilson 1968).

There are three additionally relevant factors that influence both the type of policing style officers choose to adopt and how they use their discretion. The style an officer chooses is influenced by (1) his own level of desired proactivity, (2) what type of crime is a priority to the officer, and (3) his desire to promote or be assigned to a special unit.

Our argument regarding policing style is consistent with other policing style typologies.[3] For example, an officer can be an enforcer, idealist, realist, or optimist (Broderick 1987). What we explain here are important differences in police behaviors even among officers in one category, specifically the enforcer category. Enforcers believe their job is to keep the streets safe, but there are a variety of ways to achieve that goal and officers can focus on different offenses in order to feel as if they are fighting crime.[4] There is also a distinction between active and passive officers (Herbert 1998). Active officers are those who initiate more contacts with citizens, assert control, and make more arrests. The policing styles we observed are consistent with those categories. Hunters are clearly active officers at least in the dimension of initiating contacts.

Patrol officers believe responding to citizen calls for assistance is largely part of their service role and not their crime-fighting function. Officers are most proud of being crime fighters and want to practice and hone their craft. Because crime fighting is understood as self-initiated rather than citizen-requested, exploring how they spend their time when they are not responding to calls is particularly important.

As stated previously, in regards to proactive behavior, officers fall into one of three categories of policing style: hunters, slugs, or community builders. Based on observation and confirmation from officers (in discussing the performance of their peers), approximately 80 percent of Stonesville officers fell into the category of hunters and about 15 percent were slugs. In Seaside, few regular patrol officers were hunters (only about 20 percent); and most who were hunters were trying to become members of a 6 squad. In stark contrast to the Stonesville patrol officers, almost all Seaside officers would be considered slugs. They saw themselves as chiefly having the job of answering calls for service. Because there were so many different proactive units, patrol officers rarely thought it was their job to be involved in proactive work. If they did start to seriously hunt, they greatly improved their chances of being recruited to the district's 6 squads. The 6 squads, on the other hand, were 100 percent hunters. They would not have kept their positions on the 6 squad if they did not almost constantly hunt. Community builders were by far the smallest category in both cities, with only approximately 5 percent of officers providing evidence of this policing style.

Hunters were those officers who saw proactive policing as a positive aspect of their job and would devote time during a shift to make sure they did proactive work. Officers who exhibited a hunting policing style were actively looking for lawbreakers rather than waiting for a community member to identify criminal activity. During a shift, they were more likely to make resident contacts with the sole purpose of exposing criminal activity. Hunters indicated they sought felony arrests and pursued criminals because those activities were fun and exciting. Very few of the hunters we interviewed said they became police officers in order to help mediate family disputes or write speeding tickets. The "exciting" elements of police work, such as hunting drug crimes, were also consistent with the political desires of certain segments of the public. Officers respond to political pressure from the city and leadership in the department to "clean up the streets!" If the same pressure was put on stopping intimate partner violence, then officers would likewise respond aggressively in order to reduce that crime. The point is that officers are understandably responding to the public's vision of crime fighting, which also defines officers' ideals related to what types of actions make a "good" cop; in this case, the key action was hunting for "dirtbags." The two major types of crime that hunters focused on were related to drugs and stolen cars. Approximately 50 percent of hunters were most interested in finding drug crimes. Another 30 percent of hunters focused primarily on stolen cars, leaving 20 percent of hunters focused on other crimes.

The term *slug* is one used by officers themselves to describe their peers who did very little hunting. Slugs, also defined as "station queens" by Herbert (1998), are officers whose policing style involves little proactive work while staying within the parameters of institutional influences and administrative expectations. Some slugs are predisposed to avoid not only proactive work, but as much work, in general, as possible. One Stonesville veteran who would be characterized as a slug spent most of his shift driving around his assigned district, an affluent one, noting to us that there really was no crime in that part of town. The only contacts he made with the public were ones that he could not avoid. For example, when we drove by a toddler on the corner with no clothes on, he had to stop and check the child's welfare. In Seaside, some slugs did not even like to respond to calls for service. These officers would wait on responding to a call for service in the hope that another officer would respond instead. Slugs had fewer citations, arrests, and resident contacts. They were also not as valued as those who were considered hunters, because slugs did not personify the image of a crime fighter. Hunters would often refer to officers with this policing style as "lazy."

The final category of policing style observed was community building. Community builders displayed behavior that was consistent with community policing approaches. While both departments' web pages professed a commitment to community policing, especially the Stonesville web page, the line level patrol officers showed very little evidence of such a commitment. This inability or unwillingness to translate department policies into everyday actions on the job is not unique to policing: Lipsky (1980) argued that this is a problem for all street level (or line level) bureaucrats.

One of the many critiques about community policing has been the fact that communication between the administration and the line level officers creates confusion and misunderstanding for officers regarding the goals of the program (Allen 2002; Chappell 2009; Cheurprakobkit 2002; Giacomazzi and Brody 2004; Giacomazzi, Riley, and Merz 2004; Miller 1999; Patten 2010). This was seen in Seaside, where management decided to create public service areas inside of districts. Although dozens of officers were asked why the change had been made, no one really seemed to have a firm grasp on the administration's rationale. Officers thought they were engaged in community policing activities, but without clear guidance and feedback from the administration, oftentimes the officers were left in the dark regarding desired actions and the department's goals.

The issue of performance evaluations and the measurement of officer progress has been another concern with community policing (Glensor and Peak 1996; Greene and Taylor 1988; Lilley and Hinduja 2006; Patten 2010). Almost all police departments measure their officers' job performance based on easily quantifiable data: contacts, citations, and arrests. Seaside officers had to keep an activity log of their shift. Officers utilizing community policing, however, found themselves engaged in activities that were not easily quantified, which left those officers feeling underappreciated or reticent to employ community policing practices due to fear of being passed over come promotion time. Community builder officers in Seaside were very unlikely to be rewarded with a coveted team assignment, such as a 6 squad. The rare officer who adopted the community building style made contacts with people not because she thought the people were suspicious or were "dirtbags," but rather because she wanted to enhance the relationship between the police and the public. The Stonesville and Seaside administrations would likely argue their officers did not have enough time to be community builders, given staffing levels and the numbers of calls for service, but all observed officers typically had several hours of unassigned time during each shift.

One example of the work of a community builder was when a Stonesville officer, who knew there was a business that had opened up in his district, made a special trip to introduce himself to the owner and let the owner know the police department was there for him if he needed anything. The contact was perfectly consistent with the kinds of interactions community policing advocates would like to see between officers and residents. The officer was not responding to a call, he was not hunting a crime, he was simply establishing a community contact in order to help build a bridge between the community and the police. Another example was a community builder in Seaside, who started off his shift by returning to a residence he had been called to the previous day when there had been a conflict between a teenage girl and her caregivers. The officer reported to us that he had spent a lot of time with the teenager during his initial contact, and he wanted to see how she was doing the next day.

Officer-initiated resident interactions varied depending on the officer's policing style. Hunters made citizen contacts in order to find felony offenders. Slugs and community builders, on the other hand, made citizen contacts for a variety of reasons. For example, rather than stopping a car with a headlight out because the damaged headlight gave probable cause to stop the vehicle, question the occupants, and attempt to find a reason to search the car, a community builder stopped the vehicle solely in order to let the driver know about the missing headlight, and a slug might not have stopped the car at all.

Because of these different policing styles, officers approach proactive and reactive situations differently. Observations and interviews suggest, in general, hunters are *less* likely than slugs and community builders to respond to citizen calls for service with the assumption that a crime has been committed. Hunters are also *more* likely to explain to the callers that no crime has been committed and that the callers should take their issue to the civil courts or to counseling. As one hunter told us, "If I can convince the victim there was no crime, then there was no crime." En route to calls, hunters we observed would often make comments like "I wish these people could take care of their own problems" and "I'm sure it's nothing." Perhaps because of these attitudes, hunters we observed were much slower at arriving to the scene of calls for service than non-hunters. This was especially true for Seaside's 6 squads that were largely freed from answering calls for service. When they had to respond to a call, they indicated they thought it was beneath them. If the crime at issue was a misdemeanor, hunters would attempt to convince the complainant not to push for a report or an arrest. These officers explained that if there was no witness to a misdemeanor violation, they could not arrest for it. Some observed hunters even attempted to dissuade complainants by explaining that they might have to appear in court and could be held liable for the court costs if, in fact, a crime was not committed.

The distinction between hunters, slugs, and community builders is fundamental, because each style influenced the entire approach to the job. Slugs and community builders were different from hunters in other areas of their job, not only on proactive policing. Slugs, and especially community builders, were more likely to respond to citizen calls with the belief that their help was needed, and in many cases with the assumption that a crime had been committed. These officers generally had a greater sympathy for citizen callers. On the way to the scene of a call, these officers were more likely to express concern such as, "I hope no one is hurt," or "This doesn't sound good." They were also more likely to arrest when there was any evidence of a felony or when there was an individual who wanted to file misdemeanor charges at the scene of a call. Unlike hunters, non-hunters rarely attempted to convince complainants not to file misdemeanor charges.

Factors That Influence Policing Style

As previously mentioned, there are a few factors that influence an officer's choice of policing style, including, but not limited to: training, number of years on the force, field training officers (FTO), and sex. Stonesville Police Department training consists of a six-month academy and then a rigorous field-training program. Trainees have three phases of field training with at least three FTOs.[5] As the patrol officers told us, the FTOs each have their own style of policing and the recruits almost immediately see that they can also choose their own policing style. According to McNamara (1999), the style of the FTO will be reflected in the recruit's behavior. Field training includes a socialization process into the occupational code through which officers are taught what types of crimes are considered important, or "real police work," and what types are not considered important (Manning 1978; Van Maanen 1978; Stanko 1989).

In addition to the socialization process, by working with different FTOs officers are able to witness how different officers choose particular types of criminals to hunt. For example, property crimes, drug crimes, and violent offenses are all considered somewhat serious offenses by police officers, but they are not all considered good for hunting. Most violent offenses and property crimes are brought to police officers' attention by calls for service, instead.

But the main reason trainees ride with multiple FTOs during their training period is so that they are able to observe different policing styles. One FTO may have taught a trainee particular tactics for finding drug users or sellers. Another FTO may have taught her that finding stolen cars (especially if occupied) is the best part of the job because it tests all of an officer's training. This type of variety illustrates to the trainee that there is room for one's own priorities within the occupational code. It is the early decision regarding what type of cop an officer wants to be (usually when she is done riding with FTOs) that creates one's personal policing style. Once the choice of policing style has been made, officers will normally maintain that approach for at least five years. After five years, officers are considered veterans by other officers on the force and, based on our observations, are less likely to be proactive even if they had previously been hunters.

Because there was no formal FTO training in Seaside, the more senior officers did not have as much ability to shape the new officers as they did in Stonesville. For many Seaside officers, their first assignment out of the academy was on a foot beat with another rookie in a high crime area. The main proactive emphasis for the rookies was the expectation to make contacts during their shift. This may have been another reason pedestrian stops were more common than car stops in Seaside. At times, the shift commander would guide "trainees" by giving foot beat officers particular offenses to focus on, such as curfew violations, but this was not the same as formal FTO training.

Officers openly acknowledged that it was the younger officers who did most of the proactive work. Previous research has also found that younger officers are more likely to initiate more encounters (Alpert 1989) and to do so more aggressively (Alpert and Dunham 2004). Even the Stonesville Chief of Police confirmed this fact in a City Council meeting that discussed complaints against police officers. Of the proactive officer-citizen interactions that we observed, 77 percent of them were initiated by officers with less than five years on the force. Veteran officers had the reputation of merely responding to citizen calls during their shifts.[6] Essentially, it was thought that they had put their time in as hunters, so in their later years they could take it easy and become slugs. This was especially true for the line level officers because veterans who wanted to become members of a proactive squad had done enough work to get there or had been promoted in some other capacity. Some veterans had also had problems with the administration and, therefore, decided to do as little work as possible, which meant merely responding to citizen calls. We were told that some veterans had "been burned" because of something proactive they had done. For example, a sergeant had criticized an officer who conducted a search without proper cause, so this officer became less inclined to hunt. On the other hand, there were veterans who were known to still be committed to a high level of proactivity, and they seemed to have notoriety because of it. War stories were told about these particular veteran officers, which emphasized that they were the exception to the rule and were considered "true" crime fighters.

We found that part of the difference between new officers and veterans in terms of commitment to hunting could be explained by the differing expectations the administration had of those officers. Newer officers were expected to illustrate that they were crime fighters and were producing results on the job. That usually translated to their need to produce citations and arrests. The number of citizen calls an officer responded to in an evening was not, in and of itself, considered an important measure of his productivity. In Seaside, new officers understood that their activity logs could be reviewed at any time, so they made sure to demonstrate some level of proactivity during their shifts. In most cases, and this was true in both of these cities, new officers spend one year on probation during which they can be fired at any time for any reason. Rookie officers feel especially vulnerable at this stage and particularly want to impress their supervisors by illustrating they are active on the streets hunting crime as "good" officers.

Previous research is inconsistent on whether or not there are differences between male and female officers. Some studies find there are no important differences between the sexes and their policing (see, e.g., Kakar 2002; Rabe-Hemp 2008; Worden 1993), while others argue there are differences, such as their approach to community policing and their use of force (see, e.g., Brandl, Stroshine, and Frank 2001; Garner and Maxwell 2002; Miller 1999; Rabe-Hemp 2008; Schuck and Rabe-Hemp 2005). In our observations, female officers appeared to be less proactive. Of the proactive citizen-officer interactions observed, 20 percent were initiated by female officers. That number, however, is inflated by one female officer in Stonesville who made 17 percent of the total proactive stops herself. That case would seem to suggest that some female officers are much more proactive than others, but this particular officer was assigned to one of the city's primary hunting grounds, therefore, her proactivity may reflect her district more than her sex.

One female officer told us she loved her family too much "to be getting into shit." Another officer complained that she did not appreciate the officers who were out hunting drug crimes just to get a felony arrest, because going to jail to process the arrest took an officer out of his district and made it harder for the team as a whole. In general, she felt "hard chargers," or officers always out there "looking to stir things up," were not team players because they burdened the other sector officers to respond to a disproportionate number of calls for service.

Female officers typically stuck together more often than their male counterparts when they engaged in proactive activities. In general, female officers seemed to be more focused on the service aspect of the job rather than the crime-fighting aspect.[7] Research relating to female officers and their attitudes toward community policing has been mixed; some has found a positive association (Miller 1999; Schafer 2002) and some has found no difference between male and female officers (Paoline, Myers, and Worden 2000; Pelfrey 2004; Sims, Scarborough, and Ahmad 2003; Winfree, Bartku, and Seibel 1996). In our observations, even the proactive stops made by female officers were more often for societal benefit rather than simply for hunting pleasure. Stops made by female officers were often made to assist the driver rather than to "check out the driver." For example, a female officer stopped a driver to make sure the driver knew about a recall on his automobile, whereas male officers told us they strictly ran plates to see if vehicles were stolen or if the registration was expired. Our observations are similar to other research suggesting that female officers are less likely to make arrests in the presence of their peers (Novak, Brown, and Frank 2011) and are more empathetic (Rabe-Hemp 2009).

Another example of a female officer who was more inclined to be a community builder happened when she was in a Stonesville neighborhood that was typically targeted for hunting. Officer Steer saw a Black male teen kick a dog while on his bicycle. She stopped the car, got out, and talked to him. Steer told this teen that his behavior was inappropriate while she checked the computer system to see if there were any warrants out for his arrest and/or if he was on probation or parole. He was on probation and was identified as a gang affiliate. She used this interaction to try to learn more about local gang members and to encourage him to straighten out his life. She was extremely positive; she told him to go back to school and maybe even think about being a police officer one day. He seemed to appreciate the respect she showed him and the tone of the conversation was different from what we had witnessed in most other police-citizen interactions. Officer Steer was the individual engaged in 17 percent of the proactive contacts in Stonesville, but the above mentioned interaction suggests that even females who are highly proactive sometimes have different motives for their behavior. They fall more often in the style of community builders, and while male officers seem to use proactive work primarily as a crime-fighting tool, female officers use it for a variety of purposes.

Views on Proactive Work

When dispatched to calls for service, officers' typical predisposition was to assume the situation was not a criminal matter. Consequently, officers generally did not view responses to calls for service as crime-fighting opportunities. Their assumptions were not unfounded; only 11 percent of observed police mobilizations in this study involved responding to a crime. The consequence was that officers assumed callers were exaggerating the severity of situations in order to reduce call-response time, and that all suspects, victims, and witnesses lied to them. Officer after officer explained, "Everyone lies to me." Other researchers have found that officers are generally suspicious of others (see, e.g., Cullen et al. 1985; Kappeler, Sluder, and Alpert 1998; Paoline 2003).

Patrol officers have reason to believe that situations are much less dire than callers describe them to be. Citizens often call because they believe that a police presence could aid them in their situations, and not necessarily because a crime has been committed (Bittner 1990; see also the introduction of the 311 non-emergency line in Baltimore: Mazerolle et al. 2005). In one case we observed, neighbors were disputing who could put what on either side of the fence between their homes. The officer who responded explained that neither party had committed a crime, and that the civil courts were perhaps the place for them to turn if they felt there was an issue regarding who, in fact, owned the fence.

Unlike responses to calls for service, hunting was done solely for the purposes of finding lawbreakers, so it was approached as a crime-fighting activity, and one that was more likely to result in arrest. Research has indicated that different types of policing styles reflect differing rates of arrest (Chappell, MacDonald, and Manz 2006; Linn 2009; Novak, Frank, and Smith 2002). Donald Black's classic observational research project used thirty-six observers to witness over 5,713 police-citizen interactions in three cities in the summer of 1966. In Black's sample of police-citizen encounters, 13 percent were proactive, yet the arrest rate for those instances was much higher than the arrest rate for citizen-initiated contacts: approximately 50 percent compared to 62 percent. Suspects who were identified by a police officer rather than a citizen were at least 12 percent more likely to be arrested. In fact, Black (1980, 99) noted, "the police seem a bit more severe when they act completely upon their own authority than when they respond to citizens' calls." Given the interview responses and observations, this higher arrest rate is not surprising because proactive contacts are made for the *purpose and desire* to arrest. In fact, the *entire goal* of these interactions is arrest, which is what makes them so important to study. When an officer makes a proactive contact with a citizen, her assumption is that she has identified a probable "bad guy" or "dirtbag." The intent is to "find something on him," such as illegal drugs or weapons.

Black's research was completed in 1966, long before the advent of the War on Drugs. A focus on taking drugs off the street necessitates a greater level of police-citizen contact because drugs are largely found pursuant to searches. Observational studies of the police that were conducted in the early 1980s found a much higher rate of proactivity partly to meet the demands of the War on Drugs. For example, Chambliss's (1984) research of the Rapid

Deployment Unit (RDU) in Washington D.C. revealed that officers made a vehicle stop for the purposes of finding drugs, weapons, or someone wanted by law enforcement every 20 minutes throughout the shift.[8] Hunting has now expanded beyond looking for narcotics. Today, the targets for proactive police work are members of the underclass (Fagan et al. 2010). Officers are feeding less desirable people (those from the lower class) into the criminal justice system in order to maintain higher surveillance and support the cycling of people between incarceration and community supervision (Pratt 2009).

Proactivity affords a great deal of police discretion, a fact widely acknowledged by officers themselves. When asked what aspect of their job gave them the most discretion, officers said it was traffic stops or other proactive activities. The only other answer to that question was "how to handle calls," which referred to officers' choices regarding how much time was spent at the scene of a call and what type of alternative dispute resolution an officer might choose. For example, officers often separated arguing parties for the evening. In one instance, we observed two officers who resolved a situation by telling an intoxicated man, who was yelling at his mother and daughter, to go to his room for the night.

Many officers explained that their discretion was limited when they responded to calls for service, because in those cases they had to consider what the complainant and witnesses wanted done. In Stonesville, in instance after instance, officers on scenes would say to callers, "Well, tell us what you want done here." It was evident that they had been trained to ask this question, and, consequently, when we queried them, the officers confirmed they had been trained to find out how they could satisfy the citizens as a result of their service. Few Seaside officers said similar things, which, to us, indicated different training regarding citizen contacts. Overall, when officers initiated a citizen contact as compared to responding to a call for service, they had complete discretion regarding how it would proceed. In fact, officers reported they enjoyed proactive work in part because they had the most discretion in those situations.

Based on this study, an estimate of approximately half of an officer's unassigned time was devoted to proactive police work, resulting in a total of, on average, 25 percent of his time during his shift. The other half of the unassigned time was filled with completing paperwork, relaxing, and talking and meeting with peers. Based on our findings, proactive contacts, then, are important not only because they are made explicitly for the purpose of arrest, but also because officers spend a great deal of their time doing this work.

Although officers commit much of their time to hunting, the practice is not necessarily efficient. In the practice of hunting, officers have to make numerous citizen contacts in order to obtain one arrest. For example, an officer may pull over five vehicles during one shift for the purpose of finding drugs in the possession of the driver, but not make any arrests. One evening we observed an officer stop three individuals on bikes, and not one of those interactions resulted in an arrest. The officer with the greatest number of proactive contacts in one evening (six) did not make a single arrest. As mentioned previously, officers in Seaside often used pedestrian stops as a proactive tool, yet not one observed pedestrian stop resulted in an arrest. Of the 78 proactive contacts observed, only four resulted in arrests (five percent). This inefficiency is important (and discussed in more depth in Chapter 6), because it means that law-abiding citizens are being subjected to scrutiny, questions, and frisks of their persons even when they aren't participating in wrongdoing.

Targeting Dirtbags

The preceding sections illustrated how observed officers focused on particular geographic areas of the city for hunting. This section highlights the types of individuals officers contacted. Perhaps un-surprisingly at this point, individuals considered suspicious by the police are largely of the lower socioeconomic class. For example, we observed that only a few "nice" or obviously middle class cars were stopped. Every other car that was pulled over was generally in bad condition or an old model; these were cars officers would not expect a middle or upper class person to be driving. Stonesville and Seaside were a bit different on this issue, because individuals who lived in very poor areas in Seaside still likely had a "nice" car, and so other signifiers of a driver's identity were also considered in Sea-side. Cars with larger wheels, particular rims, or tinted windows were the focus of officers there, because the driver was assumed to be a racial minority. Tinted windows, in particular, were often stated as a reason for why Seaside officers stopped vehicles.

The concept of "dirtbag" or "scumbag" cars was continually re-visited in conversations with officers. The following are some ex-amples of what officers described. Each quote is from a different officer.

> "I make stops of cars, not people."
> "We are trained to identify cars that people on drugs would
>   be driving."
> "Good car stops are those that have dirtbags in them."
> "I stop beat-up cars."
> "You can tell the kinds of cars drug dealers drive."
> "If you see an old rusted out bucket [an old car in poor
>   condition] with three or four unwashed, gnarly looking
>   folks, you have to stop it. Most likely everyone has a
>   warrant. We call those cars 'warrant wagons.'"

One observed officer came across an old white car with White teens in it, and he said that it would be a good stop. When asked why, he responded, "Because it is a car with young kids in it, and it's a beat-up old car. I'm criminal profiling." Another officer reported that old Oldsmobiles were good cars to stop because "dirtbags" usually drove them.

In Stonesville, any car that was in poor condition or "beat-up" was considered suspicious. It was these vehicles that most often had their plates run and were most often the ones considered likely to be occupied by criminals. Officer Stevens explained that he would run a plate of a vehicle, "if the person doesn't look like he should be driving that car." Another officer explained that he stopped beat-up cars "for things hanging off their rearview mirror or for a cracked windshield [in order] to look for dope." Hence, the traffic stop would not be because of a traffic code infraction, but rather because the officer thought an occupant of a "beat-up" car was suspicious, and he *used* the vehicle infraction as a reason to stop the individual. In other words, it would be a pretext stop.[9]

The Supreme Court decided the use of pretextual vehicle stops was constitutional in *Whren v. United States* (1996). Justice Scalia, delivering the opinion for the unanimous court, held that an officer's motives for a particular stop were irrelevant. All that was of concern was whether probable cause for the vehicle stop existed or not. If an officer had probable cause to stop a vehicle because of a traffic violation, it was not an infringement on the driver's Fourth Amendment rights, even if the officer's motive was unrelated to enforcing the traffic code.

In Seaside, a hunting traffic stop of a Vespa began with a Black male making a right hand turn. The officer, who was a member of a 6 squad, said: "Oh, let's make that stop. I think maybe he didn't use his turn signal." The driver was pulled over, and the vehicle was found to have several bags of marijuana in it. The driver was taken into custody, and the 6 squad members transported him to the Central facility. In order to sidestep any claims of racial profiling by the driver, the officer who had initially made the stop stated it was this kind of stop where you wanted to be sure to write a traffic ticket. The legitimacy of the initial police stop would be scrutinized less by a defense attorney if there was also a traffic citation accompanying the stop. Even though pretext stops are legal, this officer felt the legality of his stop was more legitimate with a traffic citation.

A total of three officers were involved with this arrest. Two of them appeared to be in agreement and talked briefly about the potential infraction. The third officer, however, said to the detainee, "Don't worry, man. We're not going to give you a ticket." At that point, one of the other officers, who was visibly irritated by this statement, crumpled up the ticket he had started to write.

Though the above example was of a traffic stop in Seaside, pedestrian stops were also a common tactic for 6 squad officers. In those instances, officers consistently justified the stops by referencing the type of neighborhood they patrolled. In only one other case was additional rationale offered: "I think that guy looks familiar." In over 110 hours of observation in Seaside, there was not a single observed pedestrian stop of a White person, even though the city's population was approximately 40 percent White.

In reaction to public outcry about racial profiling, one officer told us that he was not able to see the race of drivers, but "instead you look at the type of car they're driving and if it's the type of car a scumbag would drive, then I find a reason to pull it over." The officer went on to say, "I can always find a reason to pull over a car. We are trained to identify cars that people on drugs would be driving." When this Stonesville officer was asked whether he received this training from the academy or from the FTOs, he responded he was taught such techniques during his field training when his FTO would point out to him what types of cars should be targeted for traffic stops.

Hunting Drugs

Our research found that officers who hunt for drug crimes tend to make a greater number of vehicle, bicycle, or pedestrian stops than officers who do not hunt for drug crimes. Drug crimes are extremely hard to find by merely responding to citizen calls, making these crimes almost purely hunted offenses. The inability to search for drugs after making a vehicle, bicycle, or pedestrian stop would make drug arrests almost impossible.

The usefulness of bicycle stops for hunting drugs may not seem obvious. Because Stonesville is a California city with relatively mild weather, people can ride bicycles for transportation most of the year. Stonesville officers explained that they liked to stop bicycles because it was easy to establish probable cause for stops and bicycles were often used by individuals "in the system." Bicycles, in general, are easy to stop because their riders often do not realize they need to follow all the rules of the vehicle code. Bicycle-riders, therefore, often make mistakes such as not coming to a full stop at stop signs or not riding in the direction of vehicle traffic. Also, officers explained that people on bicycles in Stonesville were most likely on probation or parole and were riding a bicycle because their driver's license was revoked. People on probation or parole were desirable contacts because they were likely to be on searchable status, which means they could be searched by any law enforcement professional that contacts them, even without cause (see Chapter 5).

During Stonesville observations, we saw many bicycle stops. One such example came when Officer Vine told us he was going to drive through a "known" high-drug area that had a park that attracted drug dealers. As we were driving down the street, the officer saw a Black male on a bicycle and said, "Ah, now that's a good stop." Vine had just explained that he liked to make bicycle stops because the cyclists "usually [had] drugs on them." Once he pulled over the rider for not stopping at a stop sign, we approached him and could immediately see numerous tattoos on his arms. Law enforcement officers often use tattoos to identify individuals who have most likely served time in prison or who are members of a gang. Vine asked the man if he was on probation or parole. The man responded that he was on parole, and so the officer searched him, found a few individually packaged bags of marijuana, and took the suspect into custody.

Vine behaved in a way that was typical of those officers we observed who made it a priority to find drugs. As researchers have argued, there is a link between the War on Drugs and citizen searches (Chambliss 1984, 2001; Engel and Johnson 2006; Glover, Penalsoa, and Schlarmann 2010; Gould and Mastrofski 2004; Miller 1996; Tillyer and Khlam 2011). According to past research, and our research, we affirmed that, officers who want to "get drugs off the street" tend to be more aggressive regarding making vehicle and bicycle stops as a pretext to find a way to search the car or person for drugs.

In Seaside, hunters made pedestrian stops rather than bicycle stops. In one instance, an officer took us to an area that was known as a place for people to use heroin. When people saw the officer, they ran in different directions. One individual had just taken the drug and was immobilized. The officer spoke to him in Spanish, telling him that he really should not keep shooting up and that he should think of his mother. As we continued to walk in the area, we saw three people who had chosen not to run; the officer asked them why. They said they were cooking dinner. It was lobster on an open flame! He asked if they had drugs, and they responded that they had already used them. This entire interaction was unique, though, because none of the people were frisked. In all other observed pedestrian stops in Seaside, people were frisked.

Research shows that officers' views on how different crimes affect society influence how they police and whether or not they arrest (Finckenauer 1976; Terrill and Paoline 2007). From our discussions with Stonesville and Seaside officers, it appeared the following factors influenced whether a particular officer hunted drug crimes or not. First, officers who did not hunt them often explained they thought America was losing the War on Drugs and, therefore, it was not helping anyone to arrest drug users. Veteran officers were most likely to share this sentiment. They saw the same drug users over and over again and had decided that arresting them did not solve the problem. Second, some officers felt as if drug users were merely hurting themselves and were not causing many other problems for society. For example, one officer told us she did not think drug users were a problem because they pretty much stayed at home when high, but drunk people often drove and were much more dangerous. Finally, a few patrol officers relayed that they had seen drugs around them when they were growing up and that seemed to influence how they viewed the "drug problem" as adults. For example, one officer told us, "I don't look for drugs. I think those things have to do with the way officers grew up. Drugs were around when I was a kid."

Officers who hunt drugs think very differently about narcotics. For example, one told us, "Drugs are our (society's) biggest problem, which is why I go after them." Another officer explained to us that all citizen calls dealt with one of three things "sex, money, or drugs and alcohol." Because he viewed drug use as a cause for other criminal activity, he believed getting drug users off the street would reduce crime.[10] Similarly, another officer told us, "Taking a drug addict off the street is the same as taking a burglar off the street."

He explained that he believed many drug users commit burglaries to raise money for their drug habits. Interestingly, officers who held these views tended to be younger officers with fewer years on the force. They were also usually working to get as many felony arrests as they could because of their probationary status; drug arrests are viewed favorably by the administration. Another major incentive for officers to make arrests was the common understanding that arrests led to a greater likelihood of being promoted or assigned to a proactive team, which coincided with the crime fighter image.

In 1999, there were a total of 4,668 narcotics arrests in Stonesville. Three hundred and fifty six of these arrests were made by the investigative division, which leaves 4,312 arrests that were made by patrol officers. This should not be surprising, because research has demonstrated that patrol officers solve the majority of crimes (Greenwood, Chaiken, and Petersilia 1977, Horvath and Meesig 2001). Again, we found that drug arrests were almost completely hunted offenses. Although the department has a narcotics tip line, we knew of only one officer who somewhat regularly checked it and followed up on the tips in her beat.[11] Instead, most officers who hunted drugs relied on contacting people who they believed looked suspicious (i.e., dirtbags) and finding cause to search them.

In Stonesville, people suspected of methamphetamine use were regularly pointed out to us. Such individuals were most often White, dressed raggedly, had blackened teeth, and had scabs or wounds on their arms. When people met this description, they were often contacted by an officer *if* the officer was in the process of hunting or looking for someone to arrest. An example of this scenario occurred when two officers were dispatched to serve a warrant on a woman who had failed to appear in court that day. When the officers went to her home to serve the warrant, she was not at home. The person who answered the door, however, fit the description of someone who could be suspected of methamphetamine use. The officers asked if they could come in and look around for the woman they were supposed to serve. Then, rather than leaving once they were sure she was not at the residence, the officers proceeded to ask the three people present in the home whether they were on probation or parole. The officers discovered that two of the three people were on probation for possession of narcotics. After a long process of berating a man to disclose the secret stash of drugs, and telling him they would otherwise search his entire bedroom because he was on probation, the individual, who had now become a suspect, divulged the location of a small amount of methamphetamine. He was immediately arrested. What is important in this instance is that both officers considered themselves "drug hounds," and because they had initially approached the residence with the assumption they would be arresting someone, they seemed reluctant to leave before doing so. If those two officers had not made it a priority to find drugs, they would have been more likely to have departed immediately after ensuring the person they were seeking was not at home.

Methamphetamine users seemed to be the easiest to identify by sight, but crack-cocaine users, or what officers call "rock" users, also had some identifiable characteristics. Rock users, according to officers, were almost exclusively Black people with a disheveled appearance. Because rock is a stimulant, some addicts could be found out on the streets very late at night; they were unable to sleep. Officers also reported that when a person had recently smoked rock, he would have a very distinct odor, which officers call "rock breath." Hence, if an officer stopped an individual for any number of infractions and smelled "rock breath," he was likely to try to find a reason to search the person or automobile. For example, one officer we observed stopped a driver because his music was extremely loud, but when he smelled the driver's breath, he asked the driver if he could search the car, and subsequently discovered crack-cocaine.[12]

Methamphetamine and rock users, then, exhibited characteristics that made them suspect to officers. Marijuana, on the other
hand, was more often found by chance or by targeting areas where
officers had anecdotal experience with drugs being sold. There
were certain parks, for example, where officers knew drug dealers
frequented, and therefore, officers who hunted drugs would also
patrol those parks.

In Seaside, heroin was a major problem. Officers pointed out to
us public areas where heroin users went to "shoot up." Compared to
Stonesville, Seaside neighborhoods had developed very sophisti-
cated methods of alerting drug sellers and users when officers were
in the area. It was common in some districts for people to whistle
loudly when a police car was seen driving down the street. Young
children were also used as lookouts, and they would ride on a bicycle, looking for police officers in the neighborhood.

In 1999 in Stonesville, the vast majority of officers (229) made
six or fewer narcotics arrests.[13] According to these data, 437 officers made at least one narcotics arrest.[14] This statistic demonstrates that officers made, on average, no more than one drug arrest
every other month. Officers in this category were most likely not
individuals who considered themselves "drug hounds." But even
officers who were not looking for drugs would occasionally come
across them. For example, there was a man who was committing a
series of burglaries. One officer identified the suspect's vehicle and
asked for other officers to provide back up for him. When the officers entered the residence, they found the suspect in the company
of other people. An officer who was assisting at the scene searched
someone and found crack-cocaine in the man's sock. That officer
was at the scene to help bring into custody a burglary suspect, but
he ended up leaving the residence with a felony arrest for narcotics.

A second category of officers, though, consisted of individuals who were mostly hunting drug users and dealers. In 1999 in Stonesville, 191 officers made between seven and thirty-six drug arrests. These officers made at least one narcotics arrest every other month and at most three narcotics arrests per month. The final category of officers included seventeen officers who made thirty-seven or more drug arrests. These individuals were most likely narcotics detectives and a few very lucky or relentless hunters.[15] This arrest distribution is consistent with previous studies that showed a small number of officers make a high proportion of arrests (Petersilia, Abrahamse, and Wilson 1987).

Hunting Stolen Cars

Stonesville officers liked to hunt for stolen cars. While some officers attempted to learn the types of cars that were recently reported stolen and looked for those types of cars in their districts, most officers periodically entered license plates of vehicles on the street into the computer system to see if the cars have been reported stolen. This was called "running" a plate. With the advent of access to mobile data computer systems in their patrol cars, officers could check a license plate quickly themselves rather than having to call dispatch with the request. In Seaside, however, none of the observed officers were interested in finding stolen cars, but officers frequently ran plates to find out if the registered owner (RO) of the car had a suspended license. If the car's RO had a suspended license, the officers would pull over the car in hopes of a quick arrest with the ability to then search the car for drugs.

We found there are certain cars that are stolen more frequently than others. For example, at the time of the study in Stonesville, Hondas and Toyotas were the two most frequently stolen makes of cars. A couple of officers also reported to us that they thought vans were often stolen. There were also certain areas of the city that were known as dumping grounds for stolen cars. Officers who hunted stolen cars frequented those areas and the streets leading to those areas and ran as many plates as possible.

Some officers who hunted stolen cars did so because they enjoyed vehicle pursuits. According to these officers, most car thieves would attempt to outrun the police, and so a pursuit would ensue. In fact, when a car thief did not attempt to flee, the officers were disappointed that they did not get to chase him. One officer told us how she got a "hit" on a plate (meaning the car was stolen), and she got excited and identified the vehicle and its location over the radio and then "lit up" the car (attempted to pull it over). Then, she explained, "it pulled right over. I couldn't believe it." Pursuing stolen cars was seen as a task that required use of much of an officer's training. For instance, the officer in this example needed to recall pursuit policies, give a point-by-point of her pursuit over the radio, engage in tactical automobile maneuvers, talk the person out of the car once the pursuit had ended, and get the offender into custody. Officers commonly said that approaching an occupied car was the most dangerous thing they did.[16]

During our observations we saw hundreds, if not thousands, of license plates run and witnessed only one stolen car located through this method. Patrol officers who hunted cars tended to enjoy the adrenaline rush that resulted from finding a stolen automobile. Officers' interest in the excitement of stolen cars was evident in their questions of us regarding all the different things we saw after riding with other officers. Many of them wanted to know if we had experienced the chance to be in a pursuit. When we told them we had not, they always said, "Oh, that's too bad" and a few even replied, "Maybe we can get in one tonight." One officer bragged that in 1997 he had gotten into nineteen vehicle pursuits, and his clear enjoyment of it was why he still hunted stolen cars.

Officers who hunted drugs reported a similar rush when a narcotics suspect fled, however, drug suspects usually ran on foot, resulting in a foot pursuit rather than a vehicle pursuit. Drug hunters told us about how they would chase these suspects only to have the suspects throw the drugs on the ground or in bushes somewhere during the chase. In one incident, we saw three officers looking in the bushes in front of a home to locate drugs that had been thrown during a foot pursuit. In that case, the officers were successful in finding the narcotics.[17]

Supervisory Disincentives to Hunting

The practices of supervisory officers can have a very strong influence on an officer's policing style, particularly on how much she hunts.[18] As the immediate supervisor, a sergeant can especially shape an officer's hunting ability. Based on our observations, there are two ways a sergeant can impact hunting. First, sergeants who wanted their officers to repeatedly check-in and who questioned their team members created an atmosphere that decreased the desire to police proactively. Second, some sergeants were concerned about how many calls for service an officer was responsible for during a shift, because officers engaged in discretionary proactive policing might potentially have been dodging calls for service.

A climate of close management was indicated in a variety of ways. One indication was when a sergeant participated in a high degree of radio traffic. On teams that were loosely supervised, a sergeant's voice was never heard over the radio unless the situation was an extremely serious one, specifically if the call was a crime in progress or it involved a violent act. On closely managed teams though, sergeants' voices over the radio occurred on a regular basis, checking in with particular officers or asking about certain citizen calls for service.

Another indication of a closely monitored team was the degree to which officers initiated checking in with their supervisors. Officers who felt their actions might be questioned reported to their sergeants at much higher rates than their less supervised peers. The rate of checking in varied more by squad than by individual officers. In Stonesville, micromanaged squads were more often found in the South station. Rather than being entirely a result of the sergeant's personal management style, the more professional occupational culture of the South station also seemed to influence sergeants' behavior.

In Seaside, one district had a sergeant who was disliked by the officers on patrol. Officers were open in their disdain for him and the fact that they regretted having to work for him. They did not trust his oversight or how he would treat his officers if they ran into trouble while policing. Consequently, they reduced their proactive work. This was the only district we encountered where the 6 squad was disliked; this squad's members were seen as the favorite of the captain rather than as good officers who did a lot of self-initiated police work.

Finally, from time to time, closely managed squads had officers singled out by the sergeants. After roll call, sergeants would periodically ask to speak to a particular officer. This resulted in conversations among the other officers regarding why so-and-so would be treated in such a manner. We observed the development of an attitude whereby officers felt if they made a small misstep that could be construed as questionable or a mistake, they would be reprimanded by the sergeant.

This close monitoring management style reportedly reduced the officer's ability to hunt for drugs or stolen cars. Officers reported starting off the year on a new team and doing lots of proactive work and then being dissuaded from doing so because of the reaction of their sergeant. Patrol officers would say that their whole team had become discouraged by how they were supervised and had decided to take minimal risks as a result. They often said, "Why should I go out there and bust my butt just to be criticized?"

There were even officers who left the department because of a close management approach. For example, one Stonesville officer, who was known as a "hard worker" and a very proactive officer, quit after he felt he was punished for his proactivity. In one month the officer received three documented counselings (DCs) in his file, which meant a sergeant had recorded three problems with the officer and the officer was reprimanded for those incidents. According to another officer's account, the DCs were for very minor infractions, like handing in a report late (which, it was suggested, many officers do). The officer who ultimately quit felt, and his friends concurred, that the sergeant was punishing him because he was so proactive. As one of his friends noted to me, proactive contacts were risky because an officer had to "find" probable cause and make sure all of his actions were legal. Perhaps because of this caveat, some sergeants seemed to scrutinize arrests that resulted from proactive contacts. The officer who left did not end his career as a police officer; instead he made a lateral move to the local sheriff's department. At one point in Stonesville, though not during our observation period, over fifty officers had applied for a lateral move to a position with the county sheriff's department, which was at the time deemed to be more accepting of proactive behavior and more supportive of officers in general. In Seaside, several officers reported that they wished they could work in adjacent cities. Most of them cited problems with the department's policies as one of the major reasons they wanted to leave.

The second factor that seemed to decrease an officer's level of proactivity was the number of service calls received in a sector, in Stonesville, or a district, in Seaside. Perhaps even more important was the *anticipated* number of calls for service. Patrol officers continually expressed reserve about "creating things" or hunting when "the whole sector may fall apart at any minute." Officers worried about pursuing a vehicle stop or checking in on someone they knew was on probation when the rest of their team was tied up on a variety of different calls. In Stonesville, the South and East sectors seemed especially concerned that their sectors could "go to shit at any time." In Seaside's high crime districts, officers anticipated anything could go wrong in a minute. In one district in Seaside, officers joked about how many shootings they would see that shift. Because of these concerns, officers did less proactive work on Friday and Saturday nights and when there were special events occurring in the city.

Because some districts were generally considered busier than others, officers who enjoyed proactive work picked shifts and districts that allowed them enough unassigned time to hunt. For example, the officers interviewed who worked the graveyard shifts explained that they had actually requested what would appear to be a very unpopular time to work because it allowed them more time for hunting. As one officer explained it, "Only the scumbags are out between 3:00 A.M. and 6:00 A.M." According to him, it was easier to make contact with these suspicious people during this time. Another officer complained that she had moved from one area of the city to another, which resulted in decreased time to look for drugs because she was always handling calls for service, instead.

Given these reported institutional disincentives, one would expect to find a smaller percentage of proactive contacts occurring in the South sector in Stonesville. Roughly half of the proactive contacts that we observed, however, occurred in that sector, which raises interesting questions. Perhaps officers in the South sector would choose to do even more proactive work if they worked in a different climate. The South station officers often reported that they saw themselves as more professional than their counterparts in the North station. So, perhaps as a professional force, officers in the South would also expect to be engaging in a high level of proactive, crime-fighting activities. Their level of proactivity, while equal to the officers of the North station, might have been perceived as lower by officers in the South because their expectations were different. In Seaside, the officers who saw themselves as crime fighters worked to be recognized for their proactivity and reassigned to the 6 squad or other special team.

Conclusion

While the police officers we observed had the discretion to choose their own policing style, in order to be a "good" cop in the eyes of the public and their peers, officers often defaulted to a legalistic style that generally emphasizes and glamorizes arrests. This policing style was instilled in officers through their academy experience or during the FTO process. The easiest way to earn promotions and accolades was by "outperforming" other officers and accruing high numbers of arrests. Since arrests, in general, are very rare in policing, officers had to go out and seek opportunities for arrests. Officers typically hunt for drugs and stolen cars because the threshold to establish probable cause for these crimes is easier than others.

CHAPTER FOUR

HUNTING GROUNDS

And May the Odds Be Ever in Your Favor

We really need to write a ticket on this one. We don't
want people raising the issue of probable cause.
— Seaside officer

The previous chapter described officers' policing styles and
the crimes they hunt. This chapter examines where and who
officers hunt. The push to contain and control undesirable
populations occurs in a variety of ways. The police contribute to
that process through discretionary proactive policing in minority neighborhoods, targeting economically poor individuals as
likely lawbreakers. Communities and people with social power
are avoided by officers when they hunt. This behavior results in
greater surveillance of poor minorities and their neighborhoods, as
well as greater numbers of arrests of those populations for hunted
offenses. We first discuss where officers choose to hunt and then
detail what people and types of vehicles are considered suspicious
in those communities. Finally, we consider who is arrested for offenses that are almost exclusively made as a result of hunting. The
findings reflect the results of hunting — not only are minorities
and poor individuals subjected to a greater degree of police surveillance, but there are also severe consequences as a result of this
type of policing. Although extremely inefficient, hunting increases

arrest rates for the lower classes and negatively impacts relationships between the police and disadvantaged communities.

Where Proactive Policing Occurs

No matter what type of crime an officer chose to hunt, she did it in poor sections of town. No observed officer looked for criminal acts in a middle or upper class residential neighborhood. In fact, whenever officers prefaced their actions with statements like "let's go find something," they immediately proceeded to an area of town that was obviously occupied by lower class residents (characterized by run-down houses or apartments). It was in those economically depressed neighborhoods that officers stopped individuals both in vehicles and on bicycles. In Seaside, officers also made pedestrian stops. In the few instances when officers drove through middle class and upper middle class areas, they had a completely different demeanor. Instead of indicating she was looking for crime, an officer would say something like "just keeping an eye on my beat" or "just checking out the area and making sure everything is okay."

In discussing the proactive contacts observed, we cannot emphasize strongly enough how much the number of these contacts underestimates the amount of discretionary proactivity that was performed by the officers. Officers hunted for varying amounts of time prior to contacting an individual (if contact occurred at all). In both cities combined, about 52 percent of the proactive contacts were made in lower class areas of the city. Another 23 percent of the proactive contacts occurred in commercial areas in both cities. About 13 percent of proactive contacts occurred in other areas, such as city parks in both cities. The other 12 percent of proactive contacts occurred in middle class or industrial areas. There was a substantial difference in the number of proactive contacts in middle class sections between the two cities. Twenty percent of the citizen contacts were in middle class areas in Stonesville, whereas only 2 percent were in Seaside.

In none of the middle class officer-initiated contacts were the officers searching for people to stop. In other words, they were not engaged in hunting. Instead, in these situations, when an officer thought someone looked out of place or a little suspicious *for that area,* she would make contact with the citizen.[1] For example, a young man was walking alone after 1:00 A.M. at the edge of a middle class subdivision, and an officer stopped him to ask him where he was going and if everything was okay. The officer told us he questioned the man because people were not normally on the streets at that time of night in that area of town.

Officer Weber convyed the image of certain districts as fertile hunting grounds when he asked us how another officer, Officer Turner, had performed during our observations. Weber was interested in whether Turner was a "good" cop or not. When it was explained that out of all the officers observed Turner had made the most traffic stops, Weber's response was, "Well, he sure as hell should. He's in Elm Grove." The obvious indication being that Elm Grove was rife with suspects that needed police contact.

Chapter 2 noted the distinct differences between the four major sectors of Stonesville. Those differences extended to hunting opportunities. Officers saw the North sector as having a high percentage of minorities and reportedly a large number of probationers. In response, officers in the North sector made 33 percent of the observed proactive contacts. Officers also contended that the South sector was filled with citizens who knew their rights and would always assert them. Because of that belief, officers did not view the South sector as a worthwhile place to hunt, and, therefore, many hunters would not choose to work in that area of the city (only 16 percent of proactive contacts were made in the South sector). Officers believed the East sector was mostly Black and Latino, and had more unemployed residents. Almost 38 percent of proactive contacts occurred in the East sector. Downtown, or the Central sector, was described as a mix of people, because it contained business and government professionals, as well as transients and some drug activity. Approximately 13 percent of observed proactive contacts were made in the Central sector. In general, then, the East and North sectors were considered the places where the greatest opportunities for hunting existed and, unsurprisingly, 71 percent of proactive hunting occurred in these sectors.

In Seaside, the Downtown (a tourist hub) and the affluent districts on the outskirts of the city were places where less proactive work occurred. Almost half (45 percent) of all proactive contacts made in Seaside were in minority-dominated districts. As discussed in Chapter 2, due to the racial demographics in Seaside, the city had a greater percentage of racial diversity among its residents. The fact that officers in Seaside were making almost half their proactive contacts in minority-dominated districts was not necessarily cause for concern, except for the fact that the average non-White residency in these police districts was almost 90 percent. When discussed in their totality, over 60 percent of all *discretionary* proactive police contacts occurred in police districts where the percentage of non-White residents averaged 83 percent (and in none of these districts were non-Whites less than 68 percent of the population).

Although it was more convenient for the officers to hunt in their own districts so they could still quickly respond to calls for service, they did venture into other districts. One example of this situation occurred during an observation period when an officer explained he had been assigned outside his usual district. He complained that his usual district got much more activity, and he preferred his usual assignment. Hence, during the entire evening, whenever the officer had a chance, he left his assigned district and entered his preferred district to hunt. So, while a high-crime district may have had two officers assigned to it, four or five officers might have been patrolling that district. Officer Sims was one of many who confirmed our observations regarding officers hunting in other districts. She confirmed that if officers wanted to hunt and they were not in districts that were considered good for hunting, then they would go outside of their districts, and that most often they went to poorer communities outside of their districts to hunt. Sims emphasized, "Well, you can't hunt in nice neighborhoods."

Hunting Sites within Districts

Not only were particular sectors and districts sites for proactivity, officers also targeted particular streets or neighborhoods within their districts. Parks were often used as hunting grounds because of the officer perception that drug crimes were common in these areas. Transients also frequented parks, and so they were also subject to greater surveillance. While this hunting philosophy held true in both cities, the examples from Stonesville are particularly instructive.

One officer explained to us that there was a particular area, which was lower class and minority-dominated, that he thought was frequented by drug dealers, so he often went there and tried to find reasons to search people. Another observed officer, Officer Dober, discussed how certain areas of his district needed to be patrolled more heavily because of the prevalence of drug users in it. Dober drove us to one of these streets to illustrate his point. We saw three Black adults who began to run when they saw the police car, which piqued Dober's interest. Officer Dober sped up, stopped, and got out of his car to contact them. The three people crouched and hid behind another car, and Dober told them to come out with their hands raised. When they did not immediately do so, he pulled his weapon and aimed it at where they were crouching. Dober was obviously upset. The woman in the group came out before the men, and he told her to sit on the curb. The two males slowly stood up from behind the car, and he continued his commands with his gun pointed at them until he had them face down on the ground. He then put handcuffs on them and put them in the back of his vehicle. The female was told to remain sitting on the curb, and then he checked with dispatch to determine if the two males had any warrants out for their arrest. Neither of them did.

Officer Dober was convinced they had been doing drugs, and he made them submit to a variety of field sobriety tests. For example, he flashed a light in the older man's eyes and had him stick out his tongue. The interaction was filled with threats made by Dober including—"If you don't tell me the truth, I'll arrest you" and "If I see you here again, I'll arrest you." The males continued to deny they had been using drugs. Officer Dober, however, found crack pipes on both the younger male and the female, and he destroyed their pipes.

At some point Officer Dober turned to the female suspect who was sitting on the curb and said: "What am I going to do with you sweetheart?" His demeanor was completely different with her. He later explained to us that he had contacted her the previous night (which might even have been early morning because he works the graveyard shift) and had told her that if he saw her out on the streets again, he was going to arrest her. Dober asked her how long she had been up, and she replied four days. His voice was soft when he told her, "you need to clean yourself up." In the end, he let all three of them go.

Even though the interaction did not lead to an arrest, this example illustrates that discretionary proactivity can be an unattractive component of police work, because it creates disparate surveillance between different neighborhoods and groups of people. Given society's current interest in cycling undesirable populations in and out of correctional supervision, Dober's actions were consistent with this goal. The only reason the officer patrolled in this particular area was because he considered it a location to find people doing drugs. He contacted them because he thought three Black adults running across the street when they saw a police car was suspicious enough to contact them.[2] Finally, this interaction exemplified how officers approached contacts when they were hunting — people were presumed guilty of something until proven innocent.

This observation also illustrated that Officer Dober was suspicious because of where the citizens were located and the time of day. The color of their skin was also a factor in their identification as criminals, but in a much more complicated way than is often acknowledged. A well dressed Black male walking in the downtown business sector would not be immediately suspect because of his location. Place plus race, then, interact in ways that help explain why a person might be perceived as a "good stop." An example of how that might work for a White person is when one officer said: "If I see anyone White in this neighborhood, I'm going to think he's looking to buy drugs." A veteran who was policing an area of houses that cost upwards of $600,000 offered: "If I saw a Black man running in this neighborhood, I would definitely think he was up to something." Hence, regarding the phenomenon of how police officers practice proactivity, variables of race and class are not discrete separate categories. Race and class interact to influence which communities and people experience a higher level of proactivity. There was very little possibility Officer Dober was going to see any White people on that particular street. Finally, he would not have targeted *any* neighborhood if he were involved in other police duties.

Officers in Stonesville explained to us that there were certain areas of the city where they felt they had to maintain a continual presence. For example, late one night, an officer drove by a cul-de-sac and shined his spotlight into homes. He explained that officers felt like they had to periodically go into that neighborhood (in teams, because it could be dangerous, he said) to illustrate they were maintaining police surveillance of the area. Another area of the city, called F-Court, was continually referred to by police officers as an area that was completely crime-ridden. One officer said, "You couldn't walk from one end of this street to the other without being robbed." When they received calls for service in that neighborhood, officers were likely to respond in much larger groups than the normal two-officer response. The third area of the city continually mentioned was Elm Grove, again considered a high-crime area. These areas all had a high concentration of Black, Latino, and/or Asian residents.

The only time an observed officer hunted for drugs in a seemingly White area was a Black officer who said he liked to look for methamphetamines in a particular area of his beat. It did seem like the street was largely occupied by White people, but it was equally as poor and run-down as the minority areas where other officers hunted. It was evident that the officer regularly visited the area, because he knew a woman there, stopped to talk to her, and asked if she was keeping off of drugs. In general, the socioeconomic class of the neighborhood often dictated where officers hunted.

Proactive Contacts

As Skolnick (1996) argued, police officers receive a variety of inducements from their departments that lead them to arrests and citations (see also Johnson 2009; Mastrofski et al. 1994; White 2008).[3] In other words, they feel pressure to perform well on indicators that the administration values. Our interactions with patrol officers supported that conclusion. Officers talked about the statistics ("stats") they had to report to their sergeants. One officer complained that she did a good job writing thorough reports, but the department did not reward detailed report writing and instead "they want you out there looking for stuff."

The total number of proactive contacts observed was 78 out of a total of 310 contacts observed (25 percent of contacts). Still, the number of contacts severely underrepresented the amount of time spent hunting. A proactive contact often begins when an officer stops a driver for investigatory purposes. If she concludes the occupants are suspicious, the officer is likely to attempt to search the vehicle. If the driver and occupants do not appear suspicious to the officer, she is likely to give them a warning and send them on their way. The vehicle stop was not made for the purposes of giving a ticket, but instead was made because the officer was hunting for criminal activity of another sort. For example, Officer Larry told us, "I make stops looking for crooks, not really dope. I'm not into making stops for traffic enforcement. When I make a stop, I'm looking for guns, bad guys." Another example was when an officer told us, "I don't make stops for traffic infractions. That's what the 'motors' (the traffic unit) are for."[4] The exception to this was when officers wanted to be promoted to or be assigned to a special unit. Those officers knew that they needed to show "stats" or activity, so they would issue traffic tickets. They still made stops for investigatory purposes, but once a vehicle was stopped, they would likely write a ticket.

Officers we observed considered pretext stops good police work, because they could result in a narcotics or weapons arrest. Of the proactive contacts observed, 78 percent resulted in no action by the officer or, as the officers call it, the contacts were "advised," or warned. In two of the remaining instances, the officer was inclined to merely "advise," but other factors made that impossible. One of these incidents was when an officer stopped an individual riding a bicycle in an attempt to just check the citizen out, but the man "got mouthy" with the officer, which, according to the officer, resulted in the citizen getting a ticket; he otherwise would not have been cited.

Officers may like hunting, but that does not necessarily mean that proactive police work is effective or efficient. Based on our observations, an indication that vehicles were stopped because an officer was merely suspicious was the number of warnings given rather than tickets issued. This usually happened because officers wanted to see what the driver and occupants looked like and where they were going. Vehicle stops that occurred because of an expired registration, broken headlight or taillight, or cracked windshield were characterized as high discretion stops.

Fewer than 4 percent of observed proactive interactions resulted in arrests for possession of narcotics. Eighteen percent of proactive contacts resulted in traffic tickets issued, mostly for problems with the citizen's registration or for driving without a license. One citation issued was a "fix-it ticket," which meant that if the driver fixed the problem and demonstrated the correction to the court, the fee would be waived. The officer who made this stop said she was writing the ticket because the driver was White and because it enabled her to get "a quick stat stop."

Officers made proactive contacts with the desire to fight crime and find lawbreakers, yet only 5 percent of such contacts in both cities resulted in arrest. Patrol officers actively making pretext stops to find criminals, then, was largely inefficient. One such example was a team of 6 squads who decided to stop a couple of Black juveniles because "they looked familiar"; no drugs or weapons were found. Even at a 5 percent arrest rate, this figure doesn't fully reflect how inefficient hunting is, because it only indicates how many proactive contacts failed to discover criminal activity. The figure does not account for all the time the officers spent running plates, watching cars and people, and hunting before making those contacts.[5] While the practice may be inefficient if the goal is to fight crime, proactive contacts were more likely to result in some type of sanction, ticket, or arrest than were reactive contacts. Specifically, out of 232 reactive police contacts between the two cities, the police made an arrest in 3 percent (all eight arrests occurred in Stonesville) and issued some sort of sanction in 2 percent of encounters (two in each city). It is clear that proactive policing produces a similar number of arrests, but produces many more citations and frisks than interactions that are reactive or are a result of calls for service. In Seaside, of 48 proactive contacts there were 8 citations issued (17 percent) and 117 reactive contacts with 2 citations written (2 percent). In Stonesville, the numbers were very similar: there were 30 proactive contacts with 6 citations issued (19 percent) and 115 reactive contacts with 2 citations written (2 percent). Between the two cities and their reactive contacts, 11 resulted in a frisk of a suspect (5 percent), whereas the proactive contacts led to 15 frisks of a suspect (a stunning 19 percent). In and of itself, these discrepancies are not necessarily a problem, the problem, as we will see, is that the economically poor and individuals who were racial minorities, specifically poor racial minorities, were disproportionately the target of these proactive contacts.

Density and Locations of Traffic Stops

A standard defense of police departments in response to data indicating a higher proportion of minorities stopped by police is that such groups are more often suspects of crime or more often live in areas that receive a high number of calls for service (see, for example, Smith, Antonaccio, and Zingraff 2007).[6] The city of Stonesville's accounting of where traffic stops occurred illustrated that officers were not concentrating their proactive work in areas where citizens were more likely to be making calls for service. The Crime Analysis Unit of the Stonesville Police Department produced maps that illustrated the geographic density of vehicle stops and citizen calls for service.[7] Even a cursory comparison of these maps revealed that the density of traffic stops was much more concentrated than were the calls for service. In addition, there were areas of high density of traffic stops that did not correspond at all

Table 4.1. Results of Reactive Contacts

	Stonesville (%)	Seaside (%)
Number of reactive contacts	50	50
Arrests as a result of a reactive contact	7	0
Tickets issued as a result of a reactive contact	2	2
Frisks as a result of a reactive contact	6	3

Table 4.2. Results of Proactive Contacts

	Stonesville (%)	Seaside (%)
Number of proactive contacts	38	62
Arrests as a result of a proactive contact	10	2
Tickets issued as a result of a proactive contact	19	17
Frisks as a result of a proactive contact	30	13

to a high level of calls for service. For example, District 11 had many more traffic stops than citizen calls for service and had 41 percent minority residents (including Blacks, Latinos, Asians, and American Indians). A high frequency of stops also occurred in District 24, where the percentage of people at or below the poverty line was 29 percent and minorities were 30 percent of the residents. District 64 also had a high density of traffic stops and 27 percent of its population was living in poverty and 75 percent were racial minorities.

Contrary to the officers' defense, those districts that had a low density of traffic stops tended to have few minorities and poor people, but not a disproportionately low number of calls for service. For example, District 10, a district with a high number of calls for service, was 20 percent minority with only 4 percent of its residents living in poverty and had very few traffic stops. District 35, another district with a high rate of calls for service, also had a very low density of traffic stops and 6 percent of its residents living in poverty, with 12 percent of them racial minorities. Both our observations and the city's mapping, then, suggest that officers performed traffic stops in areas that were, for the most part, populated by poor and minority individuals and those stops were not clearly related to the number of calls for service in a district.

Ease of Stopping Vehicles

Officers repeatedly told us that they could pull over anyone on the street. They explained that if they only followed the vehicle long enough, the driver would do something that gave the officers a reason to stop the car. Drivers might fail to use the turn signal, not come to a complete stop, be speeding, or have defective vehicle equipment (broken taillights, headlights, license plate lights, or cracked windshields). As stated bluntly by one officer, "I can always find some reason to pull someone over if I need to." In most states it is even lawful for officers to pull over a driver that is following all the traffic laws, because it is assumed that someone who is obeying all the traffic laws is acting "suspiciously." Officer Sam talked about how broad the vehicle code was, which meant "you can always find probable cause (PC) to pull someone over." He also went on to explain that some officers did not always have PC when they stopped a vehicle, and then they would have to "come up with it" after the fact if they ended up finding drugs or weapons in the vehicle. Sam saw that as a risky way to police. He explained, "I want to have PC before I pull a car over. I don't want to have to come up with it afterwards."

In one observation of a vehicle stop, an officer was driving down the street when a truck with larger than usual tires turned quickly

out of the gas station in front of him. The driver did not cut off
the officer; he was in front of him by at least twenty yards. While the
driver turned quickly out of the parking lot, we could see from the
officer's car that there were three young Black males in the truck,
that the truck was altered (for example, the larger tires), and that it
fit the category of a "dirtbag" vehicle: it was old and in poor condition. The officer had to speed up in order to stop the vehicle. It was
not obvious why the officer had stopped the vehicle, and when we
asked him, the officer explained that he thought the truck seemed
"suspicious." The driver of the vehicle turned out to be on probation and was driving without a license. His vehicle was towed after
an inventory search was completed that resulted in neither drugs
nor weapons being found.

The Stonesville Racial Profiling Studies

Officers freely admitted that they looked for reasons to stop "dirtbag" cars, but adamantly denied that they made traffic stops based
on the race of the driver. The Stonesville racial profiling study released in 2000, as well as the much better 2008 research, however,
indicated otherwise. Officers often contended that they could not
identify the race of a driver, even if they wanted to, before they had
stopped the vehicle and walked up to the driver's door.

In direct contrast to claims that they could not identify a driver's
race, however, officers' comments made it obvious that they had
some idea of the race of the driver before they made a vehicle stop.
For example, in reference to the racial profiling study one officer
said, "I go out of my way to stop White people now. You kind of
have to." Two officers who reportedly hunted stolen cars told us
that Asians, especially Asian teens, are more likely to steal cars,
and so if they saw a car filled with Asian teens, they were going
to at least run the license plate. Another officer told us, "There is

criminal profiling. If I see four Black guys with tons of red clothes [a gang signifier], I'm going to see if I could stop them."

Officers were also quick to point out that the type of district they patrolled influenced the type of individuals they stopped. For example, if an officer patrolled a district that had a high percentage of Asians, it was likely that he would stop more Asian residents.[8] Officers often made the point that if they patrolled communities that were more heavily Black, it did not mean they were racially profiling if they stopped more Blacks. In 2000, approximately 14 percent of Stonesville residents of driving age were Black, yet they accounted for 27 percent of vehicles stopped during the racial profiling study.[9] Because officers said they had reduced the frequency with which they stopped Blacks, the number of traffic stops of Black drivers was likely higher than 27 percent before the study. As evidence of a reduction of vehicle stops, the police department during the study conducted a total of 36,854 vehicle stops. The city has historically averaged 70,000 traffic stops per year. The fact that the study *still* illustrates that Blacks are stopped disproportionate to their presence in the population reveals the occurrence of significant racial profiling in Stonesville.

The first racial profiling study in Stonesville[10] divided the city into neighborhoods based on census tracts and then compared the number of residents who were Black and over the age of fifteen in a neighborhood to the number of traffic stops of Blacks in that neighborhood.[11] Of the eighteen neighborhoods considered, only two of them had a lower proportion of Blacks stopped than found in that neighborhood. In sixteen of the eighteen neighborhoods, Blacks were stopped at a higher proportion than resided in that area. Table 4.3 is based on the first profiling study data. It shows the percentage of Black residents per neighborhood, the percentage of Black people stopped in each neighborhood, and the difference in those ratios. The average percentage of over-representation of traffic stops for the eighteen neighborhoods was 12.8. That means, on average, Black citizens were stopped at a frequency almost 13 percent greater than their representation in the city. Three communities saw traffic stops of Blacks at over 20 percent of their representation in those communities. Put differently, in the form of a rate, the overrepresentation becomes even clearer. For example, Black residents in neighborhood 9 were five times more likely to be stopped than their presence in the community would suggest. In the neighborhoods with an overrepresentation of traffic stops, the rate ranged from 5.6 to 1.1 with an average rate of 2.4.

Since our research was conducted in Stonesville ten years prior to the Seaside study, it could have been assumed the disparity in traffic stops might have declined. However, in 2008, an independent and more substantial racial profiling study was conducted in Stonesville. Instead of using a neighborhood level analysis, the researchers divided up the city and randomly selected intersections to study.[12] The results of the 2008 study unequivocally demonstrated the Stonesville Police Department was engaged in racially discriminatory traffic stops and searches after the traffic stops.

According to the 2008 study, a random analysis of traffic stops revealed both Black and Latino drivers were stopped at a higher rate than would be expected by their presence on the road. In fact, Black drivers were 2.1 times more likely to be stopped. In attempts to answer the comment that "maybe Black and Latino are worse drivers, so that is why they are stopped more frequently," the researchers also addressed the issue of "egregious violators" related to speeding (going at least fifteen miles per hour over the posted speed limit). After over 7,000 observations, the researchers concluded that White drivers were the most likely to be egregiously speeding, with Black and Latino drivers almost as likely as Whites to engage in this behavior.

Table 4.3. Overrepresentation of Black Residents in Traffic Stops in Stonesville

Neighborhood	Black Population in Neighborhood (%)	Black Drivers Stopped (%)	Over-representation (%)
9	3.6	20.3	16.7
16	6.6	19.1	12.5
11	6.9	14.8	7.9
4	7.2	22.4	15.2
12	8.6	27.7	19.1
13	10.6	30.3	19.7
15	10.6	23.0	12.4
8	11.8	20.9	9.1
14	13.3	29.7	16.4
1	15.0	38.2	23.2
3	16.5	29.7	13.2
5	21.3	41.9	20.6
17	21.7	36.6	14.9
18	24.6	33.2	8.6
6	27.1	23.2	−3.9
10	27.2	25.9	−1.3
7	27.6	49.4	21.8
18	35.1	39.2	4.1

Note: These data are from Researcher 1 (2001).

Not only were Black and Latino drivers stopped more frequently, they were also asked to exit their vehicles and subject to searches more often than would be expected. Black motorists were 1.6 times and Latino drivers were 1.9 times more likely to be asked to exit their vehicles after a traffic stop. Furthermore, Latino drivers were 2.4 times more likely to have a "Terry frisk," and Black motorists were 2.1 times more likely to be frisked if they were on probation/ parole searchable status. The "hit rates" on the searches (how frequently illegal contraband was found per search) was about the same for Whites, Latinos, and Blacks. Perhaps most interestingly, and directly related to our main argument, general patrol officers made 54 percent of the city's traffic stops, but they pulled over 64 percent of all Black motorists stopped.

These two facts directly relate to Stonesville officers' hunting of racial minorities. Even though racial minorities were not more likely to be engaged in egregious speeding, Blacks and Latinos were more likely to be stopped than White drivers. Additionally, even though Blacks and Latinos were not more likely to have contraband, both groups were much more likely to be searched than White motorists. We believe that the hunting of specific racial groups, even when they are not more likely to be engaged in illegal activities, can have sweeping negative impacts.

The frequency and targeted nature of discretionary proactive contacts influences reactive contacts. A climate of resentment is created, which results in a lack of cooperation with, and respect for, police officers. As far back as the 1967 President's Commission on Law Enforcement, it was acknowledged that "aggressive preventative patrol" created tensions between minority communities and the police. There is a long documented history in the United States that has demonstrated the negative relationships between minority communities and the police (Bayley 1968; Chu and Hung 2010;

Fridell et al. 2001; Skolnick and Fyfe 1993; Weitzer and Tuch 2006; Weitzer, Tuch, and Skogan 2008; Westley 1970).

As a recent example, in December 2011, the United States Department of Justice (DOJ) authored a blistering report that found a consistent pattern or practice of constitutional violations by the Seattle Police Department (SPD) against its citizenry.[13] The investigation was launched by the DOJ after a series of high-profiled use of force incidents and shootings by SPD officers against members of the minority community, including the fatal shooting of a homeless First Nations man. The DOJ found SPD frequently used unnecessary or excessive force, and its policies and supervision were deficient in regard to biased policing, pedestrian stops, as well as failing to consistently engage the community.

Soon after, in May 2012, Seattle experienced an extreme surge in gun-related violence in-and-around the Memorial Day Weekend, which left at least eight people dead. In fact, by May 2012, Seattle had reached twenty-one homicides; whereas the city had twenty homicides in all of 2011 and nineteen in 2010. SPD administrators and city officials were quick to blame guns and gangs for the escalated violence. In one of the shootings in the Rainier Beach section of Seattle, a predominantly Black section of the city, while police were trying to respond to the scene they were blocked by an angry crowd of up to fifty people. Some in the crowd were challenging officers to fistfights. Since the police could not control the scene, additional officers had to be called in before the medics could render aid to the victim who eventually died.

While we cannot draw a straight line between the SPD's excessive and unnecessary force and the increasing contempt shown by certain members of the minority community toward SPD officers, it is a reasonable conclusion. One man, speaking about the strain between the Seattle community and the SPD officers, stated in part:

"What I've learned is there is such a disdain for the system and the police that some people would rather see a killer go free [then help the police]."[14]

In the most recent Gallup Poll (2004) on racial profiling, 53 percent of Americans believe that racial profiling by police is widespread. Sixty-seven percent of Black respondents, and 63 percent of Latinos, believe that police racial profiling is endemic. In general, Black citizens have a less favorable view of their local police than do their White counterparts. In 2008, only 12 percent of Blacks and 30 percent of Latinos had a great deal of confidence that their local law enforcement treated Blacks and Whites equally (Gallup Poll 2008). Weitzer and Tuch (2002) found individuals who had been victims of racial profiling (both Black and White) were dissatisfied with the police and believed that racial profiling occurred.[15] Middle class and better educated Blacks were also more likely to believe racial profiling was widespread and to say that they had experienced it (Weitzer 2000; Weitzer and Tuch 1999). Webb and Marshall (1995) also found that class affected attitudes toward the police. In general, research shows that experiences with the police affect citizens' attitudes toward officers (Cheurprakobkit 2000; Schafer, Huebner, and Bynum 2003; Worrall 1999).

Arrest Indicators

Higher levels of police contact with certain people raises questions regarding the effects of increased contact. Our research shows that residents who were contacted by police as a result of hunting were more likely to be sanctioned than those contacted because of a call for service. In this section we consider arrests that Stonesville and Seaside officers made almost solely resulting from hunting, specifically narcotics and drug paraphernalia arrests.

To examine the differential impact of hunting on arrests, U.S. Census data was used to determine demographic characteristics of the police districts, and then we compared that information to 1999 narcotics arrests.[16] Drug offenses, in general, are almost exclusively a hunted offense because typically officers must identify citizens who appear suspicious and find a reason to search them in order to make a drug arrest. As Ward (2002) noted, evidence for greater policing of minorities can be found in examining arrests for crimes that are not "openly visible," because they must be made as a result of a stop or proactive contact.

In Stonesville, being arrested for drugs was most strongly correlated with people living at or below the poverty level in any given district. Percent at or below the poverty level is a very important and interesting variable for our purposes because race and the situation of being poor cannot be disaggregated when we are discussing how communities are policed. The 65 percent correlation between living at or below poverty level and being arrested for drugs indicates that poor districts are subjected to a higher level of surveillance and, therefore, are more likely to have higher numbers of drug arrests (Table 4.4). Conversely, income of a district is negatively correlated with the number of drug arrests, meaning districts with a higher mean income level witnessed lower levels of narcotics arrests.

The correlation between being a minority and being poor has been well documented (Carter, Schill, and Watcher 1998). The connection between race and poverty was reflected in both cities, as well.[17] Correlations for the districts in Stonesville (by percent White, Black, Latino, and other minority) confirmed the connection and the results were as expected. For example, the percent minority in a district (Latino, Asian, American Indian, and Black) is correlated with percent at or below the poverty level at 56 percent at a significance level of 0.01. The correlation between percent minority in a district and percent at or below the poverty level was even stronger in Seaside at 66 percent at a significance level of 0.001.

Table 4.4. Most and Least Narcotics Arrests and District
Demographics in Stonesville

	Poverty (%)[a]	Minority (%)
Most Narcotics Arrests		
District 24 (474)[b]	29.0	29.6
District 61 (415)	37.0	82.0
District 22 (381)	22.1	28.6
District 23 (333)	31.2	35.2
District 60 (314)	25.2	54.2
Least Narcotics Arrests		
District 10 (20)	3.5	20.1
District 32 (43)	24.4	53.2
District 43 (44)	5.8	46.8
District 36 (54)	5.5	10.8
District 11 (58)	6.5	41.2

[a] The city's overall poverty rate was 13.7%.
[b] Number of arrests in parentheses. Presented from most to least arrests
and vice versa.

A comparison of the areas with the most and the fewest narcotics arrests also illustrates the complicated nature between the intersection of race and socioeconomic class. In 1999 in Stonesville,
District 10 had the fewest narcotics arrests — twenty (four Black).
District 10 was also 80 percent White with a median income of
$34,092. Not only was it the district with the fewest narcotics ar-
rests, it also had the lowest level of poverty at 4 percent (the city as
a whole had a poverty rate of 13.7 percent). District 24 had the most
narcotics arrests, 474, which is an enormous difference compared
to District 10 (+454). District 24 had 29 percent of its residents at

Table 4.5. Correlation between Arrests and Percent of District at or Below the Poverty Level in Stonesville

Arrests	N	Pearson's r
Narcotics	4,522	0.654[a]
Paraphernalia	1,068	0.652[a]
Marijuana	898	0.376[b]
Methamphetamine	1,232	0.535[a]
Cocaine	762	0.629[a]
Prostitution	184	0.498[b]

[a] Significant at the 0.01 level (two-tailed)
[b] Significant at the 0.05 level (two-tailed)

or below the poverty level, a median income of $15,032, and was 30 percent minority. Another good example that illustrates the connection between race and class is District 61, which had 415 narcotics arrests, with 37 percent of its population at or below the poverty level and 82 percent of the district a racial or ethnic minority (see Table 4.4).

In Stonesville, when each narcotics offense is considered separately, the correlation between arrests and poverty persists. As shown in Table 4.5, correlations were found between poverty level and marijuana (0.376), methamphetamine (0.535), and cocaine (0.629). In examining particular drugs, we would expect some correlation with race or ethnicity. Percent in poverty in a district had a much closer relationship to methamphetamine arrests than did percent White. Unfortunately, cocaine arrests is a complex variable because the California penal code does not distinguish between powder cocaine, which is typically considered a White person's drug, and crack cocaine, which is generally thought to be a minority person's drug. For the most part officers told us that

Table 4.6. Correlation between Arrests and Percent of District
at or Below the Poverty Level in Seaside (2010)

Arrests	N	Pearson's r
Narcotics	19,695	0.220
Marijuana	7,184	0.562[a]
Heroin	2,526	0.229
Crack	5,019	0.698[b]

[a] Significant at the 0.01 level (two-tailed)
[b] Significant at the 0.001 level (two-tailed)

the people they arrested were using "rock," or crack cocaine, not
powder cocaine.

Much like Stonesville, Seaside experienced similar correlations
between arrests and poverty, but with some notable differences.
In Seaside, there is no data collected on methamphetamine. According to officers, that particular drug is not a problem in the
city. Conversely, according to officers, there is a very high level of
heroin use in Seaside. Correlations were found between percent at
or below the poverty level and marijuana (0.562) and crack cocaine
(0.698). Additionally, there were also strong correlations between
percent minority in a district with above 50 percent and arrests for
possession of marijuana (0.599) and crack cocaine (0.611) both significant at 0.01 (Table 4.6).

In 1999 in Stonesville, District 24 had the most methamphetamine arrests, at 133. Given what the officers reported regarding
race and methamphetamine use, it was expected this district would
have a high percentage of Whites. According to the 1999 census,
District 24 was 70 percent White. The district also had a very high
level of poverty (29 percent) and a median income of $15,032. These
facts illustrate the complexity of discretionary proactive police

work. In order to understand where officers are spending their time hunting for drugs, poverty and race must be considered simultaneously. For example, a district that had a high percentage of minorities would not necessarily be a site for proactivity. A district could have many minorities who are financially successful and, therefore, it would not be viewed by officers as a high crime area. Instead, a district that had both a high level of poverty and a high percentage of minorities was likely to be considered by officers as a good place to hunt, such as District 61 in Stonesville.

District 61 had the most cocaine arrests, at 125. Minorities made up 82 percent of this district, which suggests officers were probably arresting for the possession of crack cocaine more often than powder cocaine. The percent at or below the poverty level of this district was high, at 37 percent. In fact, District 61 had the second highest number of people at or below the poverty level of all the districts and also saw the largest number of prostitution arrests. In Seaside, District 22 had the most arrests for the selling and possession of crack cocaine (almost 800 arrests). Perhaps unsurprisingly, District 22's residents were 90 percent non-White. Comparatively, District 5, the district with the lowest percent of minority residents, at 13, had only 3 arrests for the sale or possession of crack cocaine (Table 4.7 and see Table 4.4).

Some conclusions can be drawn from a citywide look at who the Stonesville and Seaside police officers arrested for narcotics offenses. In Stonesville, Black citizens were disproportionately arrested for narcotics offenses. In 1999, Blacks were only 16 percent of the Stonesville population, yet they accounted for 39 percent of the total narcotics arrests. Other minorities did not seem to share the same dismal fate. Latinos were 21 percent of the population and made up 18 percent of the narcotics arrests. Whites and Asians were arrested for narcotics offenses at a lower rate than they were found in the city. Whites were about 50 percent of the population

4.7. Most and Least Narcotics Arrests and District Demographics in Seaside

	Poverty[a] (%)	Minority (%)
Most Narcotic Arrests[b]		
District 25 (3,018)[c]	48	76
District 22 (1,886)	46	90
District 19 (1,420)	24	86
District 35 (1,357)	25	94
District 12 (1,261)	28	93
Average	34	88
Least Narcotic Arrests		
District 5 (37)	13	11
District 7 (39)	22	11
District 6 (215)	40	20
District 9 (307)	24	15
District 1 (475)	43	25
Average	29	16

[a]The city's overall poverty rate was 25.1 percent.
[b]District 23 and 24 were collapsed during data collection making it impossible to determine the number of arrests combined with the correct census data.
[c]Number of arrests in parentheses. Presented from most to least arrests and vice versa.

and only 40 percent of narcotics arrests, and Asians were 17 percent of the population but only accounted for 2 percent of narcotics arrests. In Seaside, we see a very similar trend targeted toward the Black community. While the Black and White residents each accounted for 40 percent of the population, Blacks suffered a dispro-

Table 4.8. Drug Arrests in Stonesville and Seaside

	Stonesville	Seaside
Drug arrests by race (%)	40 (White)	67 (Black)
	39 (Black)	17 (Latino)
	18 (Latino)	15 (White)
	3 (Asian)	1 (other)
Disparity of drug arrests by race compared to population in the city (%)	−10 (White)	+27 (Black)
	+23 (Black)	+5 (Latino)
	+3 (Latino)	−25 (White)
	−14 (Asian)	−2 (other)

portionate 67 percent of all drug arrests compared to Whites who were only represented in 15 percent of drug arrests. Latinos were slightly overrepresented by their drug arrests, with 17 percent of arrests, and only 12 percent of the population (Table 4.8).

A comparison of the rates of narcotics arrests between the races illustrates the disparities created by discretionary proactive policing. In 1999, for every 1,000 Black males in Stonesville, 50 were arrested for a narcotics offense. Yet, for every 1,000 White males, only 10 were arrested for a narcotics offense. Black women incurred the same arrest rate as White men (10 in 1,000). White women in Stonesville had an arrest rate of half that of Black women.[18] Such rates also suggest the complexity of the relationships between sex and race in interactions with the criminal justice system.

Districts 43 and 11 in Stonesville are examples of why the percent minority in a district is not the only variable that is important to consider. Both of these districts had high percentages of minorities (48 and 41 percent respectively), but very few narcotics arrests by comparison: a combined total of 53. They also both had high proportions of Asians who made up a large portion of the total percentage of minority. District 43 was 27 percent Asian and District 11 was 10 percent Asian. Asians in California, however, are a diverse ethnic category. Chinese, Japanese, and Koreans are, for the most part, faring better economically than the Hmong and Laotian residents. According to officer and newspaper reports, Hmong and Laotians are also more likely to be members of gangs, when compared to the Chinese, Japanese, and Korean residents. Perhaps, then, the high level of minorities in districts 43 and 11 do not trigger police proactivity because of their racial breakdown. If the Asian component is taken out of the minority percentage, that means district 43 and 11 have 20 percent and 31 percent combination of Blacks, Latinos, and American Indians respectively. Neither one of the districts have a high level of poverty, which helps demonstrates that it is the combination of a high level of poverty and high percentage of minorities that fosters high levels of proactivity in a district.

District 32 seemed to go completely contrary to the trend. It had both a high level of poverty and a high level of minorities, however, it is located in the heart of downtown. District 32 includes the major downtown shopping plaza, a pedestrian mall, and government buildings. Both data and our observations showed that it was full of a variety of types of people at all times of the day and night. On a single street an officer could find a transient, a white collar worker, a drug dealer, and a schoolteacher. Officers did not hunt much in the downtown area for two major reasons. First, as one officer explained, "officers are afraid of stopping a normal person," because that person would be more likely to question the stop and file a complaint with the department. Second, because of the number of transients in the downtown area. If officers stopped a person on the street and then realized that he was a homeless person, according to one officer, most officers would say something like, "Oh, geesh. Can you just not put your hands in your pockets until I can get my gloves on?" She elaborated, "You just don't even want to touch them." Seemingly, then, when someone arrives at a certain destitute level of poverty, he becomes a less desirable target for hunting. Only four observed proactive contacts occurred in District 32, confirming officers' reluctance to hunt this downtown area.

Although District 32 was an anomaly regarding the number of arrests compared to the level of poverty and high percentage of minorities, the behavior of officers within the downtown area confirmed our larger points rather than refuting them. Officers, for the most part, did not make proactive vehicle stops in the downtown area because it was harder to identify "dirtbags" there. They considered District 32 to be filled with "normal" people and, therefore, determined that it was not a great site for proactive work. This phenomenon suggested that if officers were not able to focus on poor individuals or vehicles, they were less inclined to engage in proactive work.

Racialized Interactions

We live in a society where the issue of race is still salient in everyday life and discourse. Like all of us, police officers have to work within this societal framework. In our observations, occasionally the topic of race would be inserted into the police/citizen encounter, regardless of whether the contact was proactive or reactive. The officers were then often forced to either defend themselves or explain their behavior, even if the officers were responding to a call for service instead of making a proactive contact. Since officers almost exclusively hunted in poor and racial minority-dominated communities, their contacts with residents were influenced by their hunting and residents often came to resent the police. While officers categorically denied that race influenced their decision-making processes in any way, there were subtle influences of racialized interactions.[19] The examples below demonstrate how the concept of race was, at times, intertwined with the decisions of the officers we observed.

One example occurred when a major electronic supply store

called the police department to request an officer to come in and fill out the paperwork for a citizen's arrest of three youths who had been caught stealing by the store's security cameras. The officer who was assigned to the call, Officer Barrios, explained that the company had a no-discretion policy that required that everyone who was caught stealing be criminally pursued. On our way to the electronics store Barrios checked the computer system for the three youths, to see if there were any warrants out for their arrests. He explained to us that this tactic was common, because officers wanted to know more about the perpetrators before they arrived on the scene.[20]

When we entered the security office, we saw a White male employee in his late teens or early twenties sitting behind a desk, working on the papers for the arrests. On the other side of the desk there were three Black young men and one Black woman. She introduced herself to Officer Barrios as the mother of two of the boys. Barrios began to explain to her what he was doing. He said that, as a first step, he was waiting for dispatch to let him know if any of the boys had outstanding warrants. She replied, "Why, because they're Black?" Barrios began to shout, "Why? Did I say that? Did I say that?" She responded, "No." He then told her that she should wait outside, because she was obstructing the performance of his job. He repeated this statement a few times, and she said that there was no way she was leaving her children. Barrios finally relented and dropped his demand for her to leave the room.

When the theft was confirmed, the mother questioned why the boys had to be cited for misdemeanors for the theft of something worth a mere twelve dollars. The employee responded incredulously, asserting that the boys had to be held responsible for their actions. Barrios neither tried to mediate this conflict, nor did he try to reduce the sting of the employee's criticism. He did, however, give the boys a harsh lecture that included the fact that they should feel sorry for embarrassing their mother. He, of course, had realized this was an issue for her after hearing her repeat to the boys, "How could you do this to me?"

After this interaction was over, Barrios indicated to us that he probably would not have issued the misdemeanor arrest if it was solely his discretion. He would have had the youths put the items back and go on their way. We asked him what he thought of the interaction with the mother. Barrios said he was angry, because she had basically called him a racist. His opinion was that officers need to take control of a situation, and he felt that he was doing that by asking her to leave, but when she refused, he said he decided not to push the issue. The mother, however, was outraged because she suspected the officer was making decisions based on the race of her boys. Such tensions often lead to problems between the police and citizens.

In another instance, the police department received a call after dark that a large group of people were gathered at a park attached to a school, and alcohol was involved. Three officers responded to the situation and explained to the group, approximately forty Black residents of the community, that the park had closed at dusk. While there was evidence of some beer cans, the people were largely barbecuing and playing games. It was a picnic, and there were many families involved. The residents resented being ordered to disperse. Some of them questioned whether the officers would demand that they leave if they were White people gathered in Zoo Park (located in an affluent area of the city). Many yelled at the officers, expressing that they felt they were being treated unfairly. Later we asked an officer what he thought about the comparison to Zoo Park patrons. He said that people who lived around Zoo Park knew they were not allowed to be in the park after dark, so the police would not have had to tell them to leave.

Another example of a racially charged incident was when officers were called to a street in which women were reported to be fighting. Officers arrived on the scene to see dozens of Black teenage girls yelling at one another. There were a few adults on the scene who the officers talked to and asked to help keep everyone calm. The young women carried on yelling and generally seemed to ignore the officers and other adults. The girls' incessant arguing seemed to irritate the officers. The officer we were riding with left the scene with the comment, "They're animals."

Officers were called back to the location of the fighting teens two more times that evening. The second interaction was similar to the first, with more serious threats from the officers this time. One officer told the adults that if officers had to return another time, people were going to be arrested. On the third visit the officers decided that words were having no effect, so they used a different tactic to clear the streets. Three officers parked their patrol cars in the street and held down their bullhorns. The sound was deafening. They kept the noise going until almost everyone had left the street. It became clear, however, that one woman was not going to leave, and that she wanted to speak with an officer. After at least ten minutes of this deafening noise, the officers finally stopped the bullhorns and came out of their cars, visibly annoyed.

The woman said she was the mother of one of the girls who had been involved in the arguing, and she wanted to know how to file a complaint. Both the mother and the officers appeared exasperated with each other. The officers said her daughter had previously been the aggressor. The mother denied this assertion and criticized the officers for not coming out of their cars sooner in order to speak with her. In the end, the incident was resolved when the officers gave the woman the information she needed about how to file a complaint. Once everyone had left the scene, one officer stated, "Ever since Rodney King, I'd rather get in trouble for doing nothing. Since Rodney King, whenever we come out, it's like they want to get us involved in a fight. Get us involved in some way."

This interaction occurred on a street that appeared to be home to primarily middle class citizens. The houses were larger, with three and four bedrooms, and were generally well kept. The residents of the homes were Black. The bullhorn technique the officers used was, no doubt, offensive and disruptive to neighbors, but the officers showed no reluctance in using it. Based on the totality of our observations, officers would not have used the bullhorns as they did in a middle class White area or upper class Black area. This is an example of why race and class are intertwined and need to be considered simultaneously.

Like other incidents involving Black citizens, officers repeatedly said "they" do this, or "they" are like that, as if talking about a class of people rather than the particular individuals involved. One officer who worked in an affluent district bluntly told us, "When you see a Black man running through a White neighborhood during the day, you're going to be suspicious." Another officer, who was trying to explain that officers are not racists, ironically told us, "people say cops are racists but it's not racism; it's just that these people have a ghetto mentality."

The above examples are illustrations of how the police we observed dealt with issues of race on an everyday basis. Often they were forced to manage other citizens' racism and bigotry. For example, during our observations a White female homeowner summoned the police because she did not like Blacks living next to her and, therefore, continually called the police to report supposed wrong-doing on her neighbors' part. Our argument is not that police officers are racists or bigots, but that officers work in a racialized society, and they must deal with the implications of such a social system.

Conclusion

Discretionary proactivity, then, has a variety of negative consequences. Our data, and the national trends of the last thirty years, shows a higher surveillance by the police of poor communities and people, which logically results in a greater number of arrests in those neighborhoods and demographics, particularly for crimes that are mostly hunted. As mentioned in Chapter 1, these police tactics cannot be characterized as simply racist or classist actions. There are significant nuances in the connections between class, race, discretionary policing, and the demands from the police administration on its officers that do not allow us to simply categorize officers as racists or bigots.

Proactive police work, however it is classified, creates problems for democracy because it undermines the principles of equal treatment of citizens. Furthermore, discretionary proactive police work exacerbates resentment within communities that feel they are too often the victims of zealous crime-fighting behavior. And yet, this kind of police work is completely consistent with the broader political sentiment that the poor, especially poor minorities, are a threat to society and need to be carefully monitored. The police, through hunting activities, introduce those who are considered social undesirables into a system that works to keep them constantly under criminal justice surveillance.

CHAPTER FIVE

A VICIOUS CYCLE

Re-Policing the Poor and the Effects
of Probation and Parole Status

Why would you be riding a bike? Because you're on probation
and lost your license. — Stonesville officer, on why officers
consistently stopped individuals riding bicycles

This chapter describes how the institution of policing supports the modern desire for continual criminal justice supervision of the underclasses by encouraging officers to hunt for people who are on probation or parole. According to Feeley and Simon (1992), a new penology has been created in which individuals are cycled between incarceration and probation and parole, with no apparent way out of the system. The new penology is not solely maintained by the correctional system. Instead, the police play an active role in this drama by specifically targeting social undesirables through proactive activities. A counterargument would be citizens who are on probation or parole deserve to be subjected to heightened surveillance because they have already proven they are lawbreakers. The concern, however, is that the social services used to help probationers and parolees have been diminished or in some places completely eliminated, so rather than aiding previous offenders in turning away from crime, the criminal justice system now merely targets them for increased contact, which also serves to reinforce the justification and need of the criminal justice system.[1]

When Feeley and Simon first wrote of the new penology's use of community corrections, 3.7 million adults were under some form of correctional sanction. Feeley and Simon predicted there would be an increase in the use of community corrections, because the "new penology dictates an expansion of the continuum of control for more efficient risk management" (Feeley and Simon 1992, 461). Their prediction was accurate. According to the Bureau of Justice Statistics, as of 2010, the number of individuals under some form of correctional supervision was 7.1 million while, at the same time, crime continued to decrease. Of the over 7 million under criminal justice supervision, almost 60 percent (4.89 million) are on either probation or parole (1 in 48 adults in the United States are on probation or parole).

In order to hunt and find drugs or weapons, an officer must be able to search people, their vehicles, and/or their homes. The police acknowledge this necessity and often discuss how they go about performing a constitutional search. Because citizens not under probation and parole supervision have Fourth Amendment rights against search and seizure, the police cannot harass people into a search of their persons, homes, or cars. So, instead of attempting to search the general public for contraband, the police take the path of least resistance and target individuals who are on searchable status — probationers and parolees. This chapter discusses how officers use an individual's probation or parole status as a mechanism for proactive policing tactics and examines the implications resulting from that strategy. We will see how officers clearly attempt to circumvent the spirit of the Fourth Amendment of the U.S. Constitution by isolating people who have waived their Fourth Amendment rights in order to be granted probation or parole. Officers' higher rate of searches of probationers and parolees results in discovering these individuals violating the law more often than their non-probationer and parolee counterparts. People on probation and parole are often more economically disadvantaged than other citizens (Taxman 2006) and, therefore, the over-policing of the poor is exacerbated by the focus on probationers and parolees. Searching probationers and parolees provided one of the starkest differences between policing in Stonesville and Seaside. In Stonesville, when asked, probationers and parolees were legally required to divulge their status to officers, whereas in Seaside, there was no such legal requirement. Officers in Stonesville had the ability to even more narrowly focus their discretionary proactivity towards those on probation and parole. The following sections detail the number of people on probation and parole, probationers' and parolees' diminished Fourth Amendment rights, and their lack of success at completing the terms of their community-supervised sentences. We also see how the cycle of incarceration and community supervision is affected by police behavior, specifically hunting activities.

Probation

With the dramatic increase in prison populations in the past couple of decades, courts have been using probation as a way to eliminate overcrowding (Benedict and Huff-Corzine 1997). In 2010, probationers were the largest category of individuals under correctional supervision, at 57 percent of the entire correctional population (Bureau of Justice Statistics 2010). Also in 2010, there were 4.05 million people on probation and the largest percentage of probationers had been sentenced for a drug offense (26 percent).

Probationers' lack of success, meaning their inability to complete the period of their probation without another arrest, raises questions regarding the quality of supervision or assistance. In 2006, approximately 57 percent of probationers did not successfully complete the term of their probation (Glaze and Bonczar 2007). The high failure rates by probationers and parolees, while certainly affected by poor offender choices and the work of community correctional officers, have also been influenced by the actions of police officers.

In general, probationers agree to a variety of conditions for the terms of their probation, including, but not limited to: not committing another criminal offense, not consorting with known criminals or other convicted felons (even family members), abstaining completely from drugs and alcohol, and reduced Fourth Amendment rights through the search condition. Marion County, Indiana, illustrates a typical version of the search condition: "You shall permit authorized representatives of the Probation Department or local law enforcement agencies to enter your residence and you shall submit to a search of your person, your vehicle, or your property at any time" (*U.S. v. Brown* 2004).

The Stonesville County Probation Department, like many across the nation, was and is understaffed. At the time of this study in Stonesville, in 2001, there were 14,891 adults on probation in Stones County. In Seaside County at the time of this study, in 2010, there were 21,762 adults on probation. Due to a high number of staff vacancies in both counties, thousands of probationers were unsupervised. If staffing had been at the desired level, probation officers would have supervised about 100 probationers each. In Stonesville, on average, probation officers handled anywhere from 200 to 800 probationers with a few responsible for over a thousand cases. The staffing concern was not quite so pronounced in Seaside, with the average caseload being 150 probationers. This staffing shortage meant probationers came into the office to report rather than the probation officers contacting their supervisees in their residences or at their jobs. Consequently, the probationer was usually controlling the interaction more than the probation officer, because there was no threat of surprise visits. As a result of this understaffing, with hundreds to thousands of probationers unsupervised, often the only way the probation department learned about probation violations was through new arrests. Rather than providing services and assistance to probationers, the system at the time of our observations seemed to only be providing surveillance by way of the police on the streets for the vast majority of probationers. This is a problem because police officers and probation officers have different training and supposedly different goals — enforcement versus rehabilitation.   '

Probation has traditionally been viewed as an alternative for incarceration that provides opportunities for rehabilitation.[2] Goals of probation have previously focused on employment, education, counseling, and drug and alcohol rehabilitation. Among felons sentenced to probation, drug offenses are the most common offenses (26 percent). For those probationers, theoretically, a probation officer would be focused on providing drug rehabilitation assistance for his or her client. The goal of rehabilitation, however, is undermined when probation officers do not have contact with their clients. Instead, the important current achievement of probation is that the probationer is on searchable status, which becomes a powerful tool for the police. Rather than probation serving as the rehabilitation opportunity that was originally intended, it has created an opportunity for a higher level of police surveillance for a particular population. Of course, the new searchable status is consistent with the new penology in that the new system also sees community corrections no longer as a rehabilitation opportunity, but rather as means for supervising the underclass (Feeley and Simon 1992).

Parole

Nationally, 88 percent of parolees are male, 41 percent are White, 38 percent Black, and 19 percent Latino (Bureau of Justice Statistics 2007). In 2010, there were over 800,000 parolees in the United

States and the federal parole population continued to grow, although at the state level the number of parolees has declined (Bureau of Justice Statistics 2011). Prison inmates and parolees are often painted as violent, dangerous offenders, but they are more likely to have been sentenced for a non-violent offense. In a 2007 study, 26 percent of parolees had been arrested for violent crimes, 24 percent for property offenses, 37 percent for drugs crimes, and 12 percent for other types of offenses (Glaze and Bonczar 2007). That means over 70 percent of parolees were on parole for committing a non-violent crime.

Parolees are generally educationally and economically disadvantaged. For example, the average reading level of people in prison in California is seventh grade (Legislative Analyst's Office 2008). In contrast, 62 percent of public school students in California are at or above a basic eighth grade level and 21 percent are at or above eighth grade reading proficiency (U.S. Census Bureau 2009). Prisoners' level of education is an indication that prior to incarceration it is very likely these people did not have jobs where they earned substantial incomes. Not only are parolees released from prison largely undereducated, they also do not have many skills or much family support (Petersilia 2000). Most prisoners are released with no financial savings, the inability to collect unemployment benefits, and minimal job opportunities.

As is typical nationally, California parolees are largely unsuccessful in completing the terms of their parole; most of them return to prison either for a new offense or for violating parole. In 1999, Stonesville County was home to 27,260 parolees and 682 parole violators were returned to prison for a new term. In California, the return rate (per 100 average daily population) with a new prison term was 13 percent, which meant a parolee had committed a new offense that resulted in a prison sentence. The return rate (per 100 average daily population) as a parole violator was 47 percent, which meant the parolee had violated some term of his parole, typically the use or possession of drugs (determined by a parole violation hearing), but was not convicted of a new offense. Interestingly, due to court rulings, California has been under mandate to markedly decrease its inmate population. In practice, the California Department of Corrections and Rehabilitation has been releasing inmates back into the custody of the local counties. Predictably, the local county jails have now become overcrowded, which has led to a statewide effort to release non-violent, non-sexual, and non-serious offenders from custody. These select offenders are still technically "in-custody" even though they are living at home, and they still are on searchable status. What this shuffling of inmates means, of course, is that in California there will now be tens of thousands of additional people subject to searches at any time for any reason.

In Seaside County, of the official information about parolees that was available, the news was slightly better. In 2010, Seaside had 11,260 parolees. There is no official data about how many of these parolees returned to prison in Seaside County, however, statewide information is available. Extrapolating from the statewide data, Seaside County would have experienced a revocation rate of almost 11 percent, or 1,043 parolees, but of the 11 percent of revocations, 64 percent were for technical violations. Nationwide, more than half of all parolees are rearrested (Petersilia 1999). Considering Stonesville officers, and California officers in general, are allowed to ask citizens about their probation/parole status, it is not particularly surprising that revocations and violations were much higher in Stones County and California.

Relinquishing Fourth Amendment Rights

Unless an inmate was sentenced to death or received a life sentence without the possibility of parole, all inmates will eventually be released back into the community. Simply translated, there are a lot of people in our communities that are and will be "searchable." One of the terms of probationers' and parolees' release is the agreement to a search condition, which allows their probation or parole officer to search them for any reason at any time. Probationers and parolees do not enjoy the same level of privacy as other citizens. The courts have largely acknowledged the constitutionality of these people waiving their Fourth Amendment rights as a condition of their probation. The rationale is the state has public safety concerns that require setting limits on the behavior of probationers and parolees and, to that end, the courts have limited probationers' freedoms (Abadinsky 2000). Generally, the courts have allowed probation searches to be conducted by *all* law enforcement officials, not just probation and parole officers.[3] Law enforcement also does not need to have probable cause or a warrant to search probationers and parolees. Their mere status of being searchable gives police the ability to search probationers and parolees during any contact.[4] This is a major factor in why parolees and probationers find it difficult to successfully complete their parole or probationary terms; in addition to generally poor decision making skills, their diminished Fourth Amendment rights have significant negative consequences for their futures in their respective communities.

An implication for giving all law enforcement wide discretion to search probationers and parolees is that proactive officers who are anxious to make felony arrests need only knock on the front doors of probationers and parolees and search their residences in the hopes of finding narcotics or weapons. Essentially, granting officers this degree of power makes targets of probationers and parolees, especially in a climate where proactive policing is valued and rewarded.

Almost every officer in Stonesville mentioned how police officers use probation or parole status to "get into" homes or cars. Proactive officers were looking to make felony arrests; and while they might have preferred hunting for particular offenses, they valued arrests for almost any felony. Officers we observed pointed out particular homes they were convinced were sites of drug dealing, and lamented that no one who occupied the home was on probation or parole, which meant they could not search the house without a warrant. They hoped that someone in the home would get arrested and be put on probation so they could easily search the residence and potentially get additional arrests. These tactics circumvent the protections provided by the Fourth Amendment.[5]

For various reasons, officers preferred to find individuals on search status rather than locate suspicious individuals and obtain search warrants. First, search warrants are only granted when officers can clearly articulate probable cause and even then the purview of their search is likely to be narrow. For example, the warrant may give the officer the ability to search a person's home, but not his car. Illustrating probable cause to a judge is not an inconsequential hurdle either. Establishing probable cause for a warrant takes a lot of time and energy that a patrol officer often does not want to expend because it will likely take him off the street and create extra paperwork. Second, officers are generally engaging in hunting when they want to search someone. If officers are out on the street looking for anyone whom they can find with drugs, they won't take the time necessary to gather information and obtain probable cause to search particular individuals. Hunting parolees and probationers is, quite simply, an efficient way to hunt, especially for drugs. Although arrests are infrequent, the ability to gather enough evidence for an arrest is increased when an officer has the ability to search a suspect.

Some Stonesville officers believed finding individuals on probation was easy in certain sectors of the city. For example, one officer said, regarding a particular neighborhood, that regardless of race, "Any dude out here [in this neighborhood] is fair game in terms of being on probation." In the course of an interaction, officers frequently asked the person contacted if he was on probation or parole. Often it was the first question after "Can I see some identification?"

While it was very common for Stonesville officers to ask people they contacted if they were on probation or parole, they only did so with people who appeared to be of a lower socioeconomic status. For example, people whose clothing were disheveled, had no shoes on, were occupants of run-down residences, or were driving older vehicles were considered to be "good stops." Not one officer asked someone who appeared to be middle or upper class if he or she was on probation or parole. In fact, when we mentioned that it seemed officers asked nearly everyone they contacted whether they were on probation or parole, an officer responded, "Not everyone. You can tell who would be on probation or parole. I wouldn't ask you, for example, because you're not the type." Those described as "dirtbags" or "scumbags," then, were the people who officers believed were likely to be on probation or parole based on physical appearance and location in the city. Additionally, officers were more likely to ask residents whom they proactively contacted rather than people they met during call for service contacts.

Not only were probationers and parolees more often contacted and searched, they were consequently more likely to be arrested. Of course, most obviously and perhaps most importantly, the greater likelihood of arrest can be explained by the fact that an officer has a better chance of finding an infraction on someone he can search than someone he cannot. Two of the twelve arrests we witnessed were the result of people being searched because they were on probation, accounting for both proactive arrests observed. Officers had no probable cause to search either individual. The officers' only justification for the search was the probation status of the individual.

There were many more probation searches that did not result in arrest (though two produced drug paraphernalia).

Officers seemed to have little patience for individuals who were "in the system." As evidence of this general observation, an officer told us, "If a person is on probation or parole, I'm probably going to arrest him." Another officer explained to us that his policy was that if the person was on probation and he found anything illegal on him or her, the officer would at least give the probationer a misdemeanor citation. The frequent recidivism of jail and prison populations illustrate the outcomes of this policing style.

Cons on Bikes

During our observations in Stonesville, officer after officer explained to us that they assumed people on bicycles had lost their driver's licenses because they were convicts and therefore had to use bicycles for transportation. This assumption became even stronger if the cyclist lacked an expensive bicycle or the typical cyclist's attire. While people who ride bicycles may be on probation or parole, people who ride bicycles may also be doing so because they cannot afford a motorized vehicle. Middle class people who appeared to be serious cyclists with expensive bicycles and helmets were not stopped and questioned by officers. One of the researchers commented to an officer that identification of people who ride bicycles as possible probationers or parolees would be an inefficient process in the researcher's hometown. Bicycling was very popular there and was how many people got themselves to work or school; the officer responded that she could tell the difference between different types of bicycle riders. She said that she would not have stopped those types of middle- and business-class people. From her perspective, and based on what we observed of the actions of many officers, any expensive bicycle gear, a helmet, or a bicycle light should be interpreted as indicators of class. As a result, officers typically drove into areas they thought had high levels of drug activity and looked to stop people on bicycles that lacked these visible indicators of middle class status.

One officer said, "Why do you ride your bike at 3:00 A.M.? Because you don't have a license because you've been in jail." Another officer told us that, "Between 12th and 21st streets there are bikers selling drugs, so I find some reason to search them." Officers sometimes followed cyclists or watched them for a period of time, waiting for them to commit a traffic infraction. Frequently, officers were looking to see if the person attempted to avoid them or if he had any gang signifiers (for example, tattoos). Of all the bicycle contacts we observed, only one ended in arrest. He was also the only individual who was on a bicycle and was searched. Perhaps unsurprisingly at this point, he was on parole.

Most of the people stopped on bicycles were not participating in activities serious enough to end in arrest (they were merely breaking the traffic code) and for the most part the stops were largely ineffective because the goal was an arrest. Usually the officer would ask the cyclist where she was going and if she was on probation. If she said she was not on probation, the officer would ask a dispatcher for a report on the individual (which would reveal whether the person had any outstanding warrants and confirm whether or not she was on probation or parole). Once the officer had the report detailing that the cyclist was in fact "clean" and there was no reason to hold her, the officer would advise her to get a bicycle light or to follow the vehicle code, whichever reason he had used to stop her. Officers were particularly fond of stopping individuals for not having a bicycle light. In fact, when we would see someone who did have a bicycle light, the officer would say, "He must have been stopped a few times for not having a light," or "He's definitely on probation or parole and doesn't want to get stopped." Ironically, in these cases, individuals being hunted were put in a position where being in full compliance of the law was also an indication of being a "dirtbag."

Recidivism and Differential Impacts

The result of police surveillance of probationers and parolees is best understood by the qualitative data relayed above, because, in general, probation contacts and searches do not result in arrests. Merely examining arrests of probationers would leave out much of the phenomenon regarding frequency and nature of contact between probationers and law enforcement. Considering rearrests of probationers in conjunction with a description of instances such as those illustrated above allows for a richer understanding of not only the increased surveillance that probationers have to deal with, but the possible effects of it as well.

Nationally, it is difficult to assess how many probationers are rearrested for a new offense, because that information is rarely collected. In 1995, 38 percent of probationers in the United States experienced a new arrest (Bonczar 1997).[6] Perhaps most telling is that over half of those arrests were made for crimes that are almost exclusively hunted, such as drug possession. Probationers were not largely arrested for offenses that began with a citizen call for assistance. Instead, probationers were arrested largely through proactive policing tactics. For example, 21 percent of probationers who experienced a new arrest were arrested for a drug offense (Bonczar 1997). The officers we observed acknowledged that the only way to locate drugs and make arrests for drugs was to be able to search suspects' bodies, vehicles, or homes.

Furthermore, 30 percent of probationers who were rearrested were arrested for public order offenses that included weapons (2 percent), obstruction of justice (2 percent), traffic violations (5 percent), driving while intoxicated (17 percent), and other such offenses (3 percent) (Bonczar 1997). These arrests are also particularly noteworthy for our argument because they encompass incidents that are highly discretionary (with the exception of driving while intoxicated). They are also offenses that most often have no victim to press charges. These types of arrests support our argument that police officers target and deal differently with probationers. Even a weapons offense is hunted; as many observed officers explained, arrests for weapons depend upon the ability to search.

Parole arrests illustrate a similar phenomenon, if not even more extreme. In 2010, California parolees had a return rate of 65 percent (included returns for both new offenses and parole violations).[7] Twenty percent of those who returned had committed a drug offense. In the state where Seaside is located, in 2010, 64 percent of returning parolees were arrested for technical violations. Again, these were arrests that likely resulted from searches of parolees' persons or property. We are not contending there is a lack of criminality among probationers and parolees, however, their criminality, especially for victimless crimes, is more easily detected and more frequently punished by law enforcement officials because probationers and parolees have no Fourth Amendment search restrictions. Clearly, there are numerous factors that help explain why only 5 percent of the general population, but 38 percent of probationers and 57 percent of parolees in California and 11 percent of the probationers and parolees in the state where Seaside is located were arrested.[8] Again, this marked disparity in recidivism is better understood by the fact that in being proactive, officers in Stonesville, and throughout California, are allowed to question people about their probation/parole status, and in Seaside officers are not permitted to do so.

Generally, most probationers receive their sentence as a result of pleading guilty to the original charge or as a result of a plea bargain. Offenders believe that probation in the community is a better alternative than serving time in jail or prison, even though a short stint of jail time does not always result in a supervised period upon release. This belief is important because an individual may choose to serve a year of probation rather than two months in jail, but this choice may lead to his inability to escape criminal justice system supervision. An individual who chose to plead guilty and be put on probation may be stopped and searched at will by the police during that term of probation, which could ultimately lead to additional charges and a longer sentence of incarceration than if the individual had served the initial jail term.

Our observations revealed an important factor that has been overlooked in attempts to understand recidivism — it is influenced by police surveillance because it is usually measured by arrests. Recidivism has been measured in a variety of ways. Maltz (1984) pointed out that defining recidivism is itself a difficult task. Researchers have examined self-reports of criminal activity, arrests, convictions, and probation and parole violations as measures of recidivism, but using arrests is the most common recidivism measure (Listwan et al. 2003; Kubrin and Stewart 2006; Ulmer 2001). This standard measurement of recidivism is suspect because it is often determined by rearrests. If researchers compared the degree of contact police officers have with probationers and parolees with that of unsupervised citizens, the differences would be glaring. As a result, recidivism rates look so high because once a person enters the system he is much more likely to be apprehended whenever he engages in lawbreaking.

The following example illustrates the detail of attention that is given to interactions with probationers and parolees. In Stonesville, Officer Globe saw a beat-up van pull up to a corner and the driver talk with someone on the street. He thought it might be a drug deal because that area was known for drug sales. Globe pulled the van over and found the passenger was on parole and that the driver was not licensed. Globe quickly put the parolee in the back of his patrol car and asked him why he was in a car with an unlicensed driver. Globe asked him a variety of other questions, including whether he was buying drugs and why he had been in prison (attempted murder was the answer). The man became somewhat disgruntled by the questions and was quickly reminded by Globe that the conditions of his parole required him to cooperate with law enforcement officials. Globe was getting angry and said, "You better not give me any lip." Other officers arrived on the scene, and they searched the van. No drugs or other illegal items were found in it. Still, Globe repeatedly insisted, "It was a good stop." Following the interaction in which the parolee was not cited or arrested, Globe, like many other officers had done previously, explained to us that he had no patience for parolees and that he would arrest parolees for any infraction.

Police behavior in proactive policing illustrates that rather than a focus on rehabilitating offenders who are supervised within the community, a system of surveillance has developed that practically ensures the probationer or parolee will experience a rearrest. The White, middle class citizen who uses powder cocaine is less likely to have been arrested in the first place and, therefore, is less likely to be on probation. The decreased likelihood of arrest is at least partly due to the fact that White, middle class drug users are less likely to buy narcotics in public areas. Even if she is sentenced to probation, as a middle class individual she is unlikely to be contacted by proactive officers as a "good stop." The result is that the poor not only are more likely to enter the criminal justice system, they are also more likely to get *stuck* in it. If a lower class drug addict is arrested for narcotics possession and then sentenced to probation, there are serious repercussions for her failure to overcome her addiction. Any future contact that she has with the police is likely to result in her arrest if she continues to use (and/or possess) narcotics.

Identifying individuals on probation is not completely random either. Officers know which districts have a higher number of probationers and parolees and they remember people they have arrested. In some cases officers do not even have to rely on their memory. They make copies of the photographs of their detainees that were taken at the jail when they were first arrested. Furthermore, officers do not necessarily have to remember arresting the individual; they only need to remember previously contacting the individual to question him regarding whether he is on probation or parole.

Half of all probationers have previously been on probation or in incarcerated, with 30 percent having been incarcerated and 42 percent on probation (Bonczar 1997). While Blumstein and Graddy (1982) found that Whites and minorities have similar recidivism rates, other researchers have found significant differences in the recidivism rates of Whites and Blacks on probation, with Blacks more likely to be rearrested (Clarke, Lin, and Wallace 1988; Irish 1989; Whitehead 1991; Benedict and Huff-Corzine 1997). Benedict and Huff-Corzine included Blacks and Latinos in their sample and found that Latinos were also more likely to be rearrested. So, what becomes most important is the first conviction, and since minorities are disproportionally arrested, the cycle of more minorities in the criminal justice system continues.

Conclusion

Our research points to police behavior and surveillance, and particularly proactive policing behavior, as factors in explaining probation and parole recidivism rates. It questions the degree to which search status leads to a greater chance of arrest when compared to the general non-searchable population. Further research is needed, however, to consider comparisons of criminal activity in the general population and the supervised population. Specifically, future research should compare self-reported criminal behavior of those who have never been arrested with those who are on probation or parole and examine the degree to which criminal activity or the level of surveillance and contact with law enforcement predicts arrests. MacKenzie and Browning (1999) have used self-report data of probationers to see if their criminal behavior was influenced by probation status.[9] Researchers should follow up such a study with a comparison to self-reported criminal behavior of those individuals who have never been arrested.

The new penology's philosophies and tactics are pervasive throughout the criminal justice system. This chapter suggests that patrol officers' proactive policing behaviors influence the continuous supervision of the underclass. Simon (1993) illustrated how the rise in probation and parole has allowed for an increase in the number of the underclass that are supervised by the system. The police also do their part by targeting the poor, including those on probation and parole, with a high level of surveillance and strict enforcement when an infraction is found.

Perhaps our findings suggest that identifying differential enforcement in America as a threat to democracy and equal protection of the law is no longer a relevant concern in this society. This "culture of control," as Garland (2001) has coined it, simply accepts and, in fact, desires perpetual oversight of individuals whom the middle and upper classes see as threats to their property and safety. The majority of Americans, especially the middle and upper classes, still balk at paying increased taxes for their ideal feeling of safety. Those considered dangerous, therefore, need to be cycled from cheaper forms of supervision (e.g., probation) to those that may cost more (e.g., prison) when the dangerous are seen as an increased risk. Hence, the cycle from community corrections to incarceration persists with the police playing an active part through proactive policing.

CHAPTER SIX

THE FUTURE

Service-Oriented Policing

*You didn't see anything! Get in the house! — comment from
mother to son when son was attempting to help police
regarding a shooting, as reported by Seaside officer*

he trend in the criminal justice system has been to continue
to put greater numbers of poor individuals under its jurisdiction often through drug laws.[1] This trend has been given
many different names: "the criminal justice juggernaut" (Websdale 2001), "the culture of control" (Garland 2001), "management
of the underclasses" (Feeley and Simon 1992), and the "waste
management model" (Simon 1993). The focus, all these authors
argue, is not on any of the traditional goals of the criminal justice
system: retribution, rehabilitation, or deterrence. The new goal of
the criminal justice system seems to be management of social undesirables, and we now understand how the police (consciously or
unconsciously) play an active part in that new orientation. Because
law enforcement personnel claim they are acting on behalf of the
safety of the masses, the public largely accepts this increased level
of control over certain segments of the population (Garland 2001;
Smith et al. 2005). A decade-long decrease in crime did not see a
corresponding reduction in levels of criminal justice supervision.
Rather, numbers of people both incarcerated and on probation and
parole have continued to rise, even though crime rates have flat-

tened.[2] With the current political climate, proactive police behaviors are understandable.

The major findings of this book document how proactive police work, or specifically hunting, occurs in a large urban context. Officers do not hunt equally in all areas of a city. There are particular places that officers would not even consider hunting, however, there are also certain areas, mainly those where lower class people either reside or frequent, in which most of the proactive work is occurring. Officers even leave their assigned districts to hunt in areas that are deemed better to find "dirtbags." If we take equal protection issues seriously, there is cause for concern that lower class residents are subjected to a greater level of police surveillance than are their middle and upper class counterparts. Equal protection guarantees extend to privacy rights, meaning the level of surveillance should also be ruled by equal protection principles. Unsurprisingly, a higher level of police presence will lead to an increased likelihood of police contact and arrest. Along with the inclination of proactive police officers to hunt in particular sections of town, it is also those people who appear to be "scumbags" who are subjected to proactive contacts.

Proactive contacts are made with the sole purpose of finding lawbreakers; and yet, such attempts are largely ineffective. Of seventy-eight observed proactive contacts, only four resulted in arrests, which correlates to a 5 percent arrest rate. Both reactive and proactive observed contacts resulted in 5 percent arrest rate, which means that proactive contacts were *no more effective* in finding lawbreakers.

Because proactive contacts rarely result in finding lawbreakers, their frequency and targeted nature suggest the result of proactivity is more akin to harassment of particular neighborhoods than an effective crime control tactic. Even judged against its own standards, to catch criminals, proactive work is unsuccessful. Hunting may not be a more effective means of finding lawbreakers, but it surely exerts the power of the criminal justice system to manage the underclass through increased surveillance.

The ineffectiveness of proactive policing calls into serious question why it continues to be practiced. Officers can hunt for hours without making an arrest or issuing a citation. Still, they continue to embrace these activities. Why? To what end? Given the expectations of the general public that the police "keep an eye" on certain people and certain communities, the police are behaving exactly as they are expected. Regardless of the number of arrests or citations issued, hunting is effective in the new penology because it keeps segments of U.S. society watched and subdued.

One of the most fundamentally problematic aspects of hunting is the fact that police officers are selecting who should be considered suspicious and more closely patrolled rather than citizens making those decisions. In a political climate that rewards the police for controlling the underclass and keeping "disorder" from the middle and upper classes, proactive policing is practiced in a discriminatory manner. Officers may not intend to make a greater number of contacts with people of color or poor people, but institutional pressures result in higher levels of policing of these populations. Again, the words of a former police officer emphasize the need for the police to saturate and harass poor and minority-dominated neighborhoods. Former Chicago police officer Juan Juarez (2004) asked his sergeant why their unit spent so much time patrolling certain economically depressed neighborhoods in Chicago. Juarez's sergeant replied, "this department, including this unit here, runs on efficiency. The only way to measure that is by the numbers. Each unit needs to qualify its existence and prove to the communities that it's doing its job" (p. 143). In explaining the disparate police harassment of poor, minority neighborhoods, Juarez's sergeant commented, "[s]hit don't change: that's the way it's always been, the way it is now, and the way it'll always be. Don't lose any sleep over the injustices, you'll get used to them; it's all just a numbers game" (p. 144). Ironically, hunting in poor and racial minority neighborhoods has been decidedly inefficient.

The percentage of proactive contacts cannot be considered in the abstract, but rather police administrators and political decision makers have to consider the degree to which proactivity (1) occurs in poor neighborhoods, (2) is focused on poor and minority individuals, (3) is focused on members of the probation and parole population who largely are not receiving rehabilitation services, (4) illustrates a focus on crime fighting rather than service providing, (5) is ineffective even if it is to be judged on the basis of a potentially useful crime-fighting tool, (6) takes officer time away from other tasks that may be more beneficial in a democratic society, and (7) alienates the communities where it is practiced.

Take yet another example from the national level that supports our data, arguments, and conclusion. The 2010 National Survey on Drug Use and Health completed by the U.S. Department of Health and Human Services contains various self-reported data from people age twelve and older about their use of illicit drugs.[3] In regards to use of illicit drugs per racial group, the report found the following: Black 10.7 percent, White 9.1 percent, Latino 8.1 percent, and Asian 3.5 percent. This data demonstrates that among Black, White, and Latino respondents, the use of illicit drugs is relatively similar (these findings have been consistent for over a decade).

When it comes to the racial breakdown of who is getting arrested for simple possession of illicit drugs, it does not match who admits to using these drugs. In 2009, according to the Federal Bureau of Investigation (FBI), over 80 percent of all drug arrests were for simple possession (not sale or manufacture or possession with intent to sell)[4] and over 45 percent of these simple possession arrests were for marijuana. In 2009 alone, Black adults accounted for 37 percent of all drug arrests. Additionally, based on the FBI's own data, the Human Rights Watch issued a report noting that from 1980 to 2007, Black adults were arrested on drug charges at rates that were 2.8 to 5.5 times higher than White adults. Granted it is impossible for us to know how many of these arrests were the result of discretionary proactive policing, as opposed to calls for service, however, based on our data and years of other empirical research, it is easy to attribute discretionary proactive policing to many of these arrests. Furthermore, by 2009, the Bureau of Justice Statistics revealed that, nationally, Black men were incarcerated at a rate that was 6 times higher than White men and 2.6 times higher than Latino men. The gap between who is using illicit drugs and who is arrested for using them is a product of many factors, one of which is discretionary proactive policing in racial minority neighborhoods.

Proactivity is not inherently undemocratic. After all, the police officers practicing it are enforcing statutes that representatives from these communities have passed. One can assume the public wants particular behaviors criminalized even if they are victimless, like using narcotics; however, how such statutes, especially victimless offenses, are enforced is made undemocratic through unequal proactive tactics. Differential enforcement, as currently practiced by discretionary proactive policing tactics, is undemocratic.

Consequences

The consequences of hunting are serious. Ever since the days of slave patrols, the Black community has had a negative relationship with the police (Hadden 2001). Black crime victims were not protected by police nor did they find justice through the help of officers. In the years following slavery, police officers stood quietly by or even participated in public lynchings (Friedman 1993). In the 1960s, police brutality against Black (and White) civil rights demonstrators was broadcasted over Americans' televisions. Since the

1990s, claims of racial profiling have been consistent and supported by various studies.[5] The relationship between the Black community and the police is simply not the same as it is and has been between the White community and the police.

Black Americans do not distrust the police without cause. History has taught them that police officers are not their allies and, in some cases, may be their enemies. Contemporary experiences have not provided the Black community with much contrary evidence, and hunting only serves to exacerbate these historical problems. When officers are looking for offenders, they search in poor neighborhoods populated with minorities. That increased surveillance and contact sends the message that poor people who are minorities are largely criminals who need to be watched for the safety of the rest of a city's residents. Goffman (2009) followed Black men in urban Philadelphia for six years. She noted that many of the men lived in paranoia and fear of the police. When the men had warrants out for their arrest (even for technical matters like curfew violations), they lived in fear of retaliation by angry or scorned lovers and family. It was not atypical for these men to be arrested at the hospital while witnessing the birth of their children.

Given these negative consequences, it becomes hard to justify hunting. Our evidence shows proactive policing is simply not more effective at finding criminals than responding to calls for service. Even if hunting as practiced had some positive results, the resulting effect on police-community relations is clearly undesirable. Hunting not only targets some communities at higher levels than others, it also undermines departments' efforts to bridge the divide between the Black and Latino communities and the police.

Problems with Current Models

The findings of our study provide us with an important context for evaluating current police models, such as aggressive order maintenance and zero tolerance policing. The particular techniques used to both solve and prevent crimes, though, may be problematic. The focus on order maintenance to reduce fear and crime in particular areas may lead to greater problems with some communities. Order maintenance and zero tolerance policing can exacerbate existing animosities by granting officers greater discretion. Community members may not embrace the police when they get a misdemeanor citation for vandalism on their own houses or for having an abandoned car in front of their own property. As yet another example of the NYPD's zero tolerance policing gone awry, Brooklyn Judge Noach Dear and his staff found that 85 percent of the drinking in public summonses were written to Blacks and Latinos, even though Brooklyn's population is 36 percent White. In response to the extreme racial disparity in citations for this seemingly trivial offense, in July 2012, an exasperated Judge Dear ruled the NYPD had to prove that in all drinking in public offenses, the alchohol content of the defendant's drink surpassed 0.05 percent — the threshold of the city's open-container law.

Strict order maintenance policing is not the answer to the problems that police departments face concerning animosities between police departments and citizens, especially minorities. None of the positive aspects of order maintenance policing seemed to be present in the everyday activities of patrol officers in Stonesville and Seaside. The norm was for officers to stay in their cars. In Seaside, officers only left their cars when responding to a call for service or when making a pedestrian stop. Officers in both cities seemed to resent citizens' attempts to talk with them. In fact, many officers complained they were annoyed when people asked them for directions or about a ticket they received from some other officer.[6] This resentment illustrates that officers still view their job as crime fighters, not as service providers.

Aggressive order maintenance policing is incredibly problematic given the findings of this study. Aggressive order maintenance is highly discretionary and largely proactive. With those features, it introduces a high risk of disparity of policing, which we have seen does not necessarily lead to higher levels of apprehension. Some would argue that order maintenance could still be successful without necessarily reducing crime if it increases citizen satisfaction and/or lowers levels of fear. But other research reviewed above should lead us to believe that such tactics have not had positive impacts on satisfaction or fear in minority communities.

Zero tolerance policing is perhaps even more problematic because there is no accompanying work to strengthen relationships with neighborhoods; instead, enforcement is highlighted. One would think that zero tolerance policing would reduce police discretion because the message is that all laws would be enforced, but that is not the case. Zero tolerance policing gives officers the authority and even encouragement to cite or arrest for low level offenses that were previously ignored. The key to the practice of zero tolerance policing is that it actually increases police discretion because with it officers have an even broader spectrum of laws to regularly enforce, but it is simply impossible for them to enforce all those laws all the time. So, who gets stopped for jaywalking? In this study we find that proactive work results in disparate impacts. Given that zero tolerance actually increases the discretion of officers, we should expect (and found) the same results.

As yet another example of how the police disproportionately targeted (and continue to target) racial minorities while hunting for crime, we return to New York City and the NYPD's order maintenance policing and, more specifically, their enforcement of the marijuana in plain view (MPV) law. The accepted theory of the NYPD has been that when violent criminals were not committing crime, they were most likely engaged in "smaller," less violent crime like smoking marijuana or drinking alcohol in public (Maple and

Mitchell 1999). So, if there was aggressive policing towards smoking marijuana and drinking in public, the police might be able to capture violent criminals in possession of firearms. All research on this topic has consistently pointed to discriminatory impacts towards Black and Latino residents (for a sample of this research please see: Fagan et al. 2010; Geller and Fagan 2010; Gelman, Fagan, and Kiss 2007; Golub, Johnson, and Dunlap 2006; 2007; Harcourt and Ludwig 2006; 2007; Johnson et al. 2008; Levine and Small 2008; Spitzer 1999).

From the mid-1990s through the early 2010s, both the nation and New York City witnessed declining and/or stable crime rates. The stop and frisk rates in New York City, however, increased over 500 percent in the same period, but these stops did not affect all citizens of New York City equally (Fagan et al. 2010). As an example, in the early 2000s, Blacks and Latinos, respectively, accounted for roughly 25 percent each of the New York City resident population, but Blacks and Latinos totaled 52 and 32 percent of all MPV arrests respectively (Harcourt and Levine 2007). Blacks were 2.7 times more likely and Latinos were 1.8 times more likely to be arrested for MPV than their White counterparts (Johnson et al. 2008). Blacks and Latinos were also more likely to be detained, convicted, and sentenced to jail for MPV compared to Whites (Golub et al. 2007). By 2006, on average, 77 of 100 Black males between the ages of 15 and 19 had been stopped by the NYPD (Geller and Fagan 2010). Even worse, Geller and Fagan reported fewer than 4 percent of these stops led to an arrest and fewer than one half of one percent uncovered a weapon. Not only were Blacks and Latinos more likely to be stopped, but the NYPD was disproportionately hunting in minority neighborhoods (Gelman et al. 2007; Levine and Small 2008; Spitzer 1999). The NYPD has continued these discriminatory stops despite the high political and social costs.

As an example, in the summer of 2012, New York City Mayor

Michael Bloomberg was forced to defend the egregious disparity of stop-and-frisks against young, Black and Latino men. Mayor Bloomberg appeared to suffer from cognitive dissonance by mentioning that the NYPD would not stop people based on their population demographics and guaranteeing that racial profiling was banned by the NYPD.

The problems with discretionary policing go much farther than the NYPD. A very cursory internet search revealed lawsuits against the following police jurisdictions for racial profiling or discriminatory policing (not use of force) that have been settled or adjudicated since 2000: Denver Police Department, Philadelphia Police Department, Cincinnati Police Department, Mount Prospect (Illinois) Police Department, New Jersey State Police, Maryland State Police, Billings (Montana) Police Department, Tenaha and Shelby County (Texas) Police Departments, and Eastpointe (Michigan) Police Department. Many of these cases were settled for tens of thousands to hundreds of thousands of taxpayer dollars. One case settled at almost one million taxpayer dollars.

Some details of the more ridiculous police tactics from the previous lawsuits: in Tenaha and Shelby County, Texas, between 2006 and 2008 it is estimated that police officers "seized" (or stole) around $3 million from motorists without any legal justification.[7] Officers would pull over drivers (almost all Black and Latino drivers) and ask them if they were carrying cash. If they were, the officers threatened to charge the motorists with money laundering or other crimes unless they forfeited their cash to the officers. In Eastpointe, Michigan, a written memorandum from the administration directed police officers to stop and question any Black youth riding his bike in any "White" area of town.[8] In many cases the boys were frisked, handcuffed, and in some cases their bikes were seized without probable cause simply for being in the wrong neighborhood.

The brief list above demonstrates that racial profiling and discriminatory policing occurs all over the United States (urban and rural, east and west, north and south, and at the municipal, county, and state police levels). The menace of *discretionary* proactive policing is ruining lives, creating hostility, and destroying trust in the police and the criminal justice system. As Judge Reuben Castillo wrote in the Mount Prospect case, profiled victims, "retain vivid memories of their police encounters for future reference" and ethnic profiling has become a "deadly cancer on our justice system."

Another of the insidious problems of discretionary proactive policing is the fact the United States is becoming more and more racially diverse. According to 2010 Census data, the Latino and Asian populations both grew by 43 percent from 2000 to 2010.[9] Latinos account for over 50 million people in the United States, Blacks for 39 million, and Asians for 15 million and the numbers of minorities are only likely to grow. The police cannot continue to harass and discriminate against these groups without causing financial catastrophe to the taxpayers that bankroll the lawsuit payments or completely eroding all faith in the criminal justice system. At a certain point in the future, the police will not be able to afford to discretionarily hunt exclusively in poor and minority neighborhoods.

Perhaps the most dedicated and overt police approach towards targeting racial minorities and engaging in racial profiling has been led in Arizona by Maricopa County Sheriff Joe Arpaio (at the time this book went to press Sheriff Arpaio was being sued by the U.S. Department of Justice and accused of racial profiling, particularly against those of Latino descent).[10] What started as "crime suppression" sweeps, appeared to quickly turn towards a targeted hunt for illegal aliens living inside the United States. With help from his deputies and posses of individuals sworn to assist the Sheriff, many claim the Maricopa County Sheriff's Office made illegal stops, searches, and seizures against citizens and legal residents that were "brown-skinned," spoke Spanish, or appeared to look or act like an "illegal alien." While living and working in the United States without proper authorization is illegal, it is not illegal to be "brown-skinned," or speak Spanish and we are not sure how one looks or acts like an illegal alien. While Sheriff Arpaio's strategy definitely caught illegal aliens, it also terrorized and angered thousands, if not tens of thousands, of law-abiding citizens.[11]

And therein lies the rub with discretionary proactive police tactics and contacting those assumed to be "criminal." While targeted and discretionary proactive patrol does catch the occasional lawbreaker from time to time, it only counts the "hits" and not the "misses." Meaning, officers and police administrators seem to forget all the times they contact "criminals" and find no criminal wrongdoing, but the one time they catch a lawbreaker, that one success obfuscates the tens or hundreds of other occasions where no illegal activity was found. These policing tactics absolutely erode public confidence in the legitimacy of the police and the entire criminal justice system. How many caught criminals through discretionary policing is it worth to have rampant mistrust from poor and minority communities, especially financially strapped minority communities?

Some of you are certainly asking, "well, shouldn't the police go to where the crime is?" Yes, absolutely. Police should respond to crime as reported by calls for service or empirically demonstrated through some sort of department-wide hot spot or COMPSTAT strategy. Some of you might also be thinking, "If the cops in your study and across the nation are going to areas known for crime and arresting criminals, that is good police work and can't be a bad thing." Wrong, it is bad. As we have demonstrated, discretionary proactive policing is inefficient and, at times, ethically dubious. Cops are wasting their time and taxpayer dollars hoping to stumble across someone committing a crime, usually a visible crime like drug possession and not a violent or serious crime that threatens public safety. Even worse, through discretionary proactive policing, the police are actively targeting the poor and racial minorities because, based on the way they look, the car they drive, the bike they ride, or where they live, these people are assumed to be criminal. Ultimately, the end result of this type of harassment is a segment of the public that no longer trusts or respects the police. For the police to be truly effective, they must have a strong working relationship with the community, the entire community. Sunshine and Tyler (2003) and Tyler and Fagan (2008) among others (Murphy, Hinds, and Fleming 2008; Tyler 2004, 2005) have found that the police gain trust by operating with fairness and procedural legitimacy. Meaning, if the police are fair in their use of enforcement, then public willingness to help the police increases. Discriminatory use of authority, such as disproportionately stopping Black and Latino residents for possession of marijuana or drinking in public, leads to public mistrust and anger towards the police.

A New Model

Instead of investing time in aggressive order maintenance police models, we argue that police departments should focus on citizen calls for service.[12] A possible advantage of focusing on citizen calls for service is this focus is inherently procedurally democratic because it relies on citizens to identify problems. Furthermore, it drastically reduces the disparity in police surveillance. In a democratic society, government agents are created to serve the will of the public equally and fairly. A consequence of hunting is that it results in officers spending their time on demonstrably ineffective strategies instead of fruitful ones. With 25 percent of an officer's time spent hunting, there is a good deal of time that could be spent on other ventures.

A reorientation of police priorities to citizen calls for service will increase the democratic nature of police departments and assist in improving their relationship with the public. Of course, part of democracy is responding to the majority's will. It is possible (if not likely) the majority of the public (especially the White populace) wants the police to engage in the crime-fighting discretionary pro-active behavior described in this book. At times, the majority has taken positions that are substantively undemocratic or discrimina-tory. According to our constitutional principles, the majority can-not infringe upon the rights of the minority, which is what is oc-curring with the current practices of discretionary proactive work.

What would a service-oriented policing model look like? Per-haps most importantly, the primary function of patrol officers would be responding to resident calls for service without going through the motions or attempting to leave as soon as possible. Calls for service would be viewed not only as a service function, but also as a real opportunity for crime fighting. Currently, officers see proactive work as their primary means of law enforcement, but citizen calls for service result in at least as many arrests (by ratio). By placing a call for service, the residents themselves have identi-fied wrongdoing and requested police assistance. Surely residents can be discriminatory as well, but it is difficult to fault an officer when he is responding to a citizen request. Another reason to view calls for service as important for crime-fighting opportunities is that most violence is interpersonal and occurs between parties known to one another (Thurman 2010), therefore, officers will have greater opportunities to deal with violent crimes when they are responding to service calls. As it is currently practiced, hunting is exclusively focused on non-violent offenses — narcotics posses-sion, weapons possession, and automobile theft.

Another aspect of a service-oriented model of policing would include genuine officer follow-up with the victim or complainant. Especially if we consider calls for service fruitful for crime fighting, then contacting the parties following the initial police response could create opportunities to gain information about suspects, issues of concern, or other problems. Since 59 percent (see Chapter 2) of police mobilizations include no citizen contact, it is typically difficult, if not impossible, for officers to know if a crime had occurred in such situations. If officers on the next shift or next day follow up at that location, it is possible they will then be able to contact a victim, complainant, or witness and ascertain if a crime had been committed and if the suspect is known.

An administrative process is necessary to identify what victims, complainants, or witnesses should be contacted after an immediate response. Currently when an officer responds to a call for service, he rarely records anything about the interaction. In a service-oriented police department, patrol officers would need to make at least brief notes as to what occurred during the contact. Officers could be provided a log sheet that simply asked them to record the time of the response, the address, the names of those contacted, and the outcome. The necessary notations should not take longer than a few minutes to record or it starts to become unlikely that officers will continue to keep the log. Another option is officers could provide the necessary information to dispatch including whether the officer recommended a follow-up visit. Supervisors could check to make sure the officer or dispatch log was being filled out for every call for service to which an officer was assigned. Using the logs, supervisors would generate daily lists of necessary contacts that each individual officer would need to make during her shift. Not every call for service would necessarily make sense for follow-up. The supervisors would decide which ones were good candidates for another officer contact. Then, during roll call meetings prior to each shift, the shift supervisor would provide each officer with the names and/or addresses of the contacts and a small amount of information about what had occurred during each first contact. The officer would be required to make all the contacts assigned to him during his shift or explain why he was too busy to do so. After attempting to meet for follow-up with the victim, complainant, or witness, the officer would then also log the outcome in a document similar to the one where he recorded initial contacts. If an arrest was made during a follow-up contact, both the arresting officer and the initial responding officer should receive administrative "credit" for the arrest.

Each department would create guidelines for supervisors to help them decide which mobilization was appropriate for another contact. If an arrest had been made during the initial response, those contacts should almost always receive a follow-up visit. The reason for this protocol is because if the case is to proceed, victim or witness cooperation is almost always necessary. A victim is especially much more likely to cooperate if she feels that criminal justice professionals will support her through the process. During this contact, the officer can also make sure that necessary resources are offered to the victim. For example, when appropriate, did the victim receive information about the local rape crisis office or some type of victim/witness assistance office? The officer can also answer questions as to possible next steps in the criminal justice process for the victim. Supervisors should also prioritize intimate partner or child abuse calls because those types of offenses are most often ongoing. Instead of simply responding to a call for service at a particular residence numerous times, officers could proactively work to help those victims. Of course, this would have to be done in a manner that is sensitive to the fact that an intimate partner violence perpetrator may punish the victim physically for accepting assistance or cooperating with police officers. At the same time, if perpetrators know that officers may come to the residence to see how the victim is doing, the perpetrator may reduce his violence or take longer to resume abuse after an arrest or contact through a call for service.[13]

A service-oriented model of policing does not rule out the possibility of proactive work, but there would definitely be less of it because officers would have the new assignment of making follow-up contact with callers and would have less discretionary time, in general. Proactive work in service-oriented policing would be guided by evidence of citizens' requests rather than by officers merely determining who they believe to be suspicious and where those individuals are likely to reside. In this way, proactive work would become targeted rather than random. A parallel can be made to the responses to the 1974 Kansas City Preventative Patrol Experiment. That study famously found that random patrol had no effect on crime rates or citizen satisfaction. As a result of that study, targeted patrol was advocated. In our study, we see that relatively random (or at least officer-determined) hunting is also ineffective in increasing arrests, and may have a negative impact on police-community relations. As a consequence, we should consider targeted hunting that is determined by citizens' priorities discovered through calls for service and tip line analysis.

One tool that was underutilized in Stonesville was the narcotics tip line. Information provided through a tip line is perfectly aligned with the underlying philosophy of service-oriented policing—residents largely identify possible law breaking and criminals, not patrol officers. Patrol officers interested in hunting for drug offenses can use these tips to target particular areas where citizens have reported suspected drug sales. Hunting locations would then be determined by citizens reporting to the tip line rather than by officers solely making that decision. Again, if calls for service are disproportionately coming from low income or minority-dominated neighborhoods, the residents are making these decisions, not the police. Under the service-oriented model, the police should go where the calls for service take them.

There are other ways to guide hunting based on evidence. As

Hickman (2010) noted in his call for more democratic policing, "[p]lace-based policing . . . focuses police efforts on places rather than people; on the context in which criminal behavior occurs, rather than the individuals involved in crimes" (p. 499). For example, crime analysis and crime mapping are fairly common in police departments today. In Chapter 4, we saw that the locations of citizen calls for service did not correlate with officer traffic stops. In particular, traffic stops were much more concentrated, suggesting that officers find particular neighborhoods preferable sites for hunting. Crime analysis will be most useful after a period of time that officers have been practicing the other aspects of the service-oriented policing model. Time is necessary because current data would reflect the results of officers' current proactive behavior. Even without the passage of time we know that only 5 percent of proactive contacts resulted in arrests, which was the exact same percentage of reactive contacts. Arrests and citizen calls for service distribution should guide where officers hunt. Because a service-oriented policing model would work to ensure that proactive policing was based on empirical guidance, there would be less concern about disparate hunting based solely on an officer's predilection of where, who, and what kinds of offenses to hunt.

In Chapter 2 we saw that officers had a general distrust of victims and a belief that victims lied to officers. A model of policing that puts responding to calls for service as its first priority and central means of crime fighting, makes victims, complainants, and witnesses officers' allies in law enforcement. Mandatory follow-up with selected callers also provides officers with opportunities to interact with callers in situations that are not as emotionally charged and are perhaps no longer crisis situations. These interactions in a more normal type of situation could work to make both officers and citizens see each other as more complex whole individuals rather than just government authority figures and victims or perpetrators.

A final benefit of the service-oriented policing model is it creates built-in oversight mechanisms that previously were not present. First, officers have to document the outcomes of their responses to service calls. Second, supervisors will review those logs in order to generate a list of follow-up assignments for the next shift's or day's officers. Third, officers may behave differently if they know that it is likely another officer will be contacting the victim, complainant, or witness sometime soon. It is common human practice to be more conscientious about work we know is likely to be reviewed by others. That is a major reason for supervisory oversight. Scholars and reformers for years have been concerned about how much of an officer's time is not only highly discretionary, but also outside of any oversight. Service-oriented policing would change that practice.

How Can the Police Proceed?

As we have seen with community policing, moving to a new model of policing is slow and difficult.[14] If service-oriented policing has a chance of being adopted, it has to take into account the organizational context of policing. Lin (2000) revealed the importance of understanding organizational context when suggesting reform. Lin examined five federal prisons and illustrated how their unique organizational contexts influenced how rehabilitation programs in prisons were implemented. She emphasized the importance of understanding, working with, and accommodating relevant actors' values and needs. Such lessons should also be considered in the context of police agencies.[15] Lin's framework would have reformers, policymakers, and researchers consider (1) what is the greatest priority to police departments, (2) what police officers value and need given their institutional goal, and (3) how specific police departments or organizational contexts influence implementation of reforms/policies. Ultimately, police departments are primarily concerned with safety, making their jurisdiction safe for the public (most specifically, the middle class public). Generally that goal translates into a focus on law enforcement and catching criminals; therefore, Lin's work would suggest that any policy that aims to reform the police should consider that overriding goal. Second, police officers themselves value crime fighting and see themselves as primarily law enforcers. The service-oriented model is not expected to be wildly popular with line level officers, particularly because it does not emphasize the intrigue and danger of policing; however, the police serve the public; the public does not need to serve the officers' egos. As community-oriented policing has increased officer job satisfaction (Adams, Rohe, and Arcury 2002; Halsted, Bromley, and Cochran 2000; Miller 1999), the service-oriented model should also increase officer job satisfaction because service-oriented policing promotes quality and repeated interactions with the public. The final consideration, organizational context, reminds us that particular police departments' organizational contexts will vary, which will necessitate development of a variety of different strategies in order to implement service-oriented policing depending on the department.

So, how would line officers be persuaded into adopting the service-oriented model? Let us be fair, police television shows and movies, while fictional, are exciting! No one goes to a cop movie to see Bruce Willis or Will Smith follow up with victims of crime to see if they need additional services. If service-oriented policing is not as sexy or exciting as discretionary proactive policing, why will line officers be willing to consider a change, even if it is demanded by the administration?

As is well known anecdotally and empirically, policing is a stressful career, especially stress relating from occupational (task-related) and organizational concerns (see, for example, Abdollahi 2002; Oliver and Meier 2004). Job dissatisfaction and lack of organizational fairness has been demonstrated to lead to high rates of depression, anxiety, aggression, and interpersonal conflict (Gershon et al. 2009). Additionally, as part of the profession, officers typically use physical and psychological domination to try and control situations and find it challenging to leave these tactics at the workplace, meaning officers take their authoritarian personality home (Johnson, Todd, and Subramanian 2005).

Discretionary proactive policing creates situations which exacerbate these job stressors for officers. Officers are contacting unknown people in unknown situations and disproportionately contacting racial minorities and the poor who feel over-scrutinized and harassed, which often leads to tense encounters where citizens behave rudely and angrily towards the officers, all because the officers feel the need to "show numbers or stats" that validate exceptionalism and worthiness to the administration. Daily encounters with angry, unreceptive citizens and a demanding administration create stressful working conditions.

In general, police officers have struggled to cope with these stresses in a healthy manner. However, stresses in police work have been shown to create elevated rates of alcoholism, intimate partner violence, suicidal ideation, and suicide (Anderson and Lo 2010; Darensburg et al. 2006; Kohan and O'Connor 2002; MacDonald, Wells, and Wild 1999; Volanti 2004), not to mention physical ailments like high blood pressure, insomnia, and headaches (Harpold and Feemster 2002). The service-oriented model can reduce these stressors and the likely resulting physical, mental, and emotional problems. The service-oriented model increases contact between crime victims and officers, increases the odds of positive contacts, and can provide officers with the feeling that they are truly helping. Instead of being burdened by statistical demands from the administration, officers can focus on the needs of victims and be true service providers. Additionally, officers will not be hampered by

end of the month ticket quotas or "performance guidelines" and
they can go wherever the calls for service demand their attention.

We are not arguing that a switch to a service-oriented model
would create a stress-free environment for officers. Rather, two of
the most potent job stressors for line officers, daily tasks and the organizational administration, would be minimized. While officers
may lose some measure of professional mystery and intrigue, they
will be gaining mental, physical, and emotional stability. As all humans seem to resist change, it is not expected that officers would
initially embrace a service-oriented model. After being presented
with the anecdotes and facts that a career in law enforcement and
the old discretionary model seem to intensify mental, physical, and
emotional problems for officers, officers may be slowly inclined to
accept a change in focus.

Police leaders who wish to move to a service-oriented policing
model would also need to reconsider their evaluation tools. Quite
rightly, officers believe that what a department values is reflected
in the "stats" they have to provide their supervisors and in the indicators used in their performance evaluations. Today, officers
continue to be evaluated on crime-fighting dimensions, such as
number of citations issued and number of arrests. Community policing reformers have consistently complained that performance
evaluations have not adapted to reflect the skills and tasks necessary in community policing (Alpert and Moore 1997; Glensor
and Peak 1996; Greene and Taylor 1988; Lilley and Hinduja 2006;
Patten 2010). Officers in a service-oriented department should be
evaluated on responses to calls for service, outcomes from follow-
up contacts, and how they have used crime analysis data to make
decisions about their behavior on patrol. If evaluation tools do not
change, then officers will continue to only see themselves as the
crime fighters current evaluations suggest they should be.

Creating the appropriate evaluation tools is extremely important and quite difficult as well. At times, what officers think is good police work might be different than the administration. Similarly, what is good policing in an urban department might be markedly different than from a suburban or rural department. Under a COMPSTAT or hotspot policing strategy, assessing crime rates, arrests, or citations may be an appropriate evaluation tool. Much like community policing, service-oriented policing is not designed nor suited for traditional quantitative measurements. In fact, as witnessed throughout this book, officers hunting to find arrestable offenses, and thus increasing their contacts quantitatively, were unsuccessful 95 percent of the time and undoubtedly were irritating and harassing the people they contacted.

So, how should a service-oriented officer (and department) be evaluated? It depends. Police professionals and scholars have witnessed the futility of trying to create a one-size-fits-all evaluation tool for drastically different types of police departments. While there needs to be some consistency so officers and departments can be compared and evaluated against each other, a service-oriented response in New York City might be completely different from one in Chico, California, but both officer and departmental tactics might be appropriate for their respective cities.

Service-oriented responses are radically different than anything the police are doing or have done in the past, so the method for evaluating them should be different. First, when officers are not responding to calls, are they revisiting residents that made prior calls for service? If the citizen was a victim of a crime, these contacts could include following up on additional information, assessing the initial police response or any services provided, providing information for other services needed, or just extending a compassionate and sympathetic ear. These contacts do not necessarily need to be long in duration, but the police can begin to eliminate the well-deserved reputation of being faceless, bureaucratic automatons. Second, if a person was not a crime victim, but simply requested police services, the officer could assess the situation and see if further action is needed and if the proper services were provided. Last, the officer could leave a "rate my service" form after the follow-up contact (the form could also be available electronically—each contact could be given a tracking number as a way of discouraging officers from padding their rates of response). Those citizens with strong enough opinions would fill out the forms, and departments could sift through that feedback to assess officer performance. The forms could contain both qualitative and quantitative information to help broaden the depth of the officer contacts. With companies like Amazon and Yelp, as well as others, all seeking people's comments after service, citizens are more used to rating others now than in the past.

Hunting is exactly what is demanded in the new penology—a greater surveillance of the poor and racial minorities, however, it is not effective or efficient as a means for crime fighting. Instead, the consequences of hunting are to feed the negative relationship between minorities and the police and to keep police officers engaged in work that is not increasing public safety. Proactive policing, as currently practiced, should fade into the past. A service-oriented policing model should rise in its stead so that time spent hunting would be utilized communicating with individuals who had previously contacted the police for assistance. Service-oriented policing would include opportunities for proactive work, but those actions would be guided by empirical evidence that highlights where officers should be spending their time.

NOTES

1. The Undiagnosed Problem

1. Interestingly, the public seems to support multiple justice goals including not only retribution, but also restorative justice goals (Gromet and Darley 2009). The criminal justice system appears not to be reflecting such support for a variety of justice goals.

2. Advocates of community policing have gradually become aware of how difficult it is for the crime-fighting culture to be overcome, but have not given up on community policing as the panacea. Miller (1999), in a very insightful book, details how issues of sex and sexuality influence the implementation of community policing.

3. See Michele Alexander's (2010) *The New Jim Crow: Mass Incarceration in the Age of Colorblindness* for an excellent explanation of how the criminal justice system is actually a racial caste system.

4. Of course, this is not to say that victims and witnesses have no prejudices of their own.

5. This "doing something" mentality is consistent with expectancy theory. See Dejong, Mastrofski, and Parks (2001) for more on patrol officers and expectancy theory.

6. Conley's (2002) focus is the pre-arrest contact of Black, juvenile males.

2. Setting the Stage

1. To ease the simplicity of reading, the personal pronoun *we* is used throughout the text. It was not possible for both authors to go on the ride alongs at the same time, so *we* refers to both of us or either one of us.

2. Due to the uniqueness of its location and population, providing any additional details would reveal Seaside's true identity. Where Seaside resides is specifically being withheld to protect the anonymity of the police department.

3. The research completed in Stonesville was part of Lori Beth Way's dissertation.

4. In comparison, when we interacted with officers in roll calls, during lunches, or when they were in other groups, they seemed slightly more guarded.

5. Research has described the boredom that patrol officers can suffer (Brown 1981), and we think having someone to talk to was welcome once they decided we were not a threat.

6. In fact, they were correct in that concern. The final report stated that twenty-five officers were significant outliers in the level of Black drivers they pulled over, but there was no context given as to which districts they were assigned.

7. The racial profiling researchers completed a small number of observations in patrol cars. Reportedly, they did so to assess whether they could identify the race of drivers and if the survey form had any problems.

8. All demographic data is based on the 2000 census because that was the most appropriate given that the research was conducted in that year. The percentages total more than 100 due to rounding errors.

9. Historically, making complaints has proven difficult, which is why there has been pressure in some cities to create citizen review boards.

10. See Pogrebin and Poole (1988) for a greater understanding of how police officers and departments use humor to reinforce institutionalized norms.

11. The term police mobilizations is used rather than citizen interactions because, as indicated, some of the mobilizations did not result in a police-citizen interaction, because no one was at the scene of the call.

12. A little over 1 percent of the observations were "attempt pick-ups" which involved officers taking individuals into custody who were wanted by the criminal justice system either for committing a crime or violating their parole.

13. There are significant concerns related with how to code an interaction a crime (see Greene and Klockars 1991). We consider mobilizations crimes when police officers consider them as such, because it is how the officers define a situation that matters most for how each interaction will be resolved.

14. The citizen interaction per hour rate was 0.76. We compared the citizen interaction rates of the North and South areas and they were almost exactly the same at 0.78 and 0.76 respectively.

15. The mean was 2.14.

16. The mean was 1.87.

17. Also, if there is more than one person in the stopped vehicle, officers will often ask for back-up so that they will not be at a numerical disadvantage.

3. Shaken or Stirred?

1. For a very brief sample of literature concerning police discretion and the mentally ill see Cooper, McLearen, and Zapf 2004; Tucker, Van Hasselt, and Russell 2008; Watson 2007. For domestic violence see Berk and Loseke 1980; Eitle 2005; Phillips and Gilham 2010. For police traffic stops and searches see Kowalski and Lundman 2007; Ridgeway 2006; Schafer et al. 2006. For race and arrest decisions see Kochel, Wilson, and Mastrofski 2011; Skogan and Frydl 2004.

2. A counter-argument is made by Klinger (1996).

3. For a broader discussion regarding police typologies see Brown 1988; Muir 1977; Paoline 2003, 2004; Skogan and Frydl 2004; Westley 1970.

4. Muir's (1977) definition of an enforcer is a bit different, because his typology was based on how comfortable the officer was with the power of coercion and the officer's perspective on the "condition of mankind."

5. Seaside does not have a FTO program. Academy training processes, however, can instill an appreciation for "real" police work and crime fighting (Bayley and Bittner 1984, Commission on Accreditation for Law Enforcement Agencies 1994; White 2008).

6. See Mastrofski, Ritti, and Snipes (1994) on how veterans prefer to avoid tasks that will create a lot of work for them and Mastrofski et al. (2000) regarding the decreased likelihood of granting citizens' requests for control of other citizens.

7. We were able to interact to differing levels with sixteen different female patrol officers and three female sergeants.

8. This unit was initially created in the 1960s in response to urban riots, but as riots were no longer a threat, the RDU was used to locate drugs. According to Chambliss (1984, 177), "For the police, the 'war on drugs' provided a functional equivalent to riots: the crisis of inner-city drugs and violence."

9. See Novak (2004) for further evidence of pretext stops.

10. See Bennett, Holloway, and Farrington (2008) for a meta-analysis on the connection between drug use and criminality.

11. Apparently, some officers think the narcotics detectives take all the "good" tips and that the ones given to patrol officers are a waste of time to investigate. Our impression, though, is that officers probably do not want to take the time that is necessary to get the tip, find the address, and complete an investigation.

12. He could have searched the car without consent anyway, because the driver's license was suspended, so the car was towed. Any time a car is towed an officer can legally search it, because an automobile with a weapon or drugs in it would be a public safety risk sitting at the tow yard.

13. The Seaside Police Department was unwilling to release information related to specific numbers of officer drug arrests.

14. There were only 242 patrol officers in Stonesville. The remaining number of officers includes detectives, special narcotics teams, and problem-oriented policing officers who were assigned to particular neighborhoods.

15. It was not possible to link one officer to every arrest. In some cases two officers who rode in the same car would receive credit for a drug arrest, but it was not possible to determine which officer actually made the arrest or initiated the contact which led to the arrest. In most instances observed, one officer took the lead in interacting with the suspect. The default practice was that the first officer on the scene took control, but there were times when a more senior officer might take on that role. The other responding officer was supportive, but generally allowed the first officer to control the scene. As observers, we could usually identify the different roles the officers played and see which officer was, for the most part, controlling the citizen interaction. This type of information, of course, cannot be accounted for in numerical data regarding how many arrests each officer made. And this challenge illustrates the importance of observational study of police decisions.

16. A few years before our research, a veteran officer of the department was killed while approaching the suspect's car. Federal Bureau of Investigation data on both officers feloniously killed and officers accidentally killed or harmed show that automobile stops are more dangerous than other activities of officers.

17. Officers who repeatedly lose foot pursuits become objects of ridicule. Someone told us about one officer who had lost three foot pursuits in a short period of time. We later rode with that officer, and he also reported the failures and told us about how he was trying to make sure he would not lose again.

18. See Engel, Sobol, and Worden (2000) for an examination of the effect of supervisory styles on patrol officer behavior.

4. Hunting Grounds

1. There was no evidence that officers were enforcing community norms as advocated by "broken windows" policing (Wilson and Kelling 1982). Officers were suspicious using their own standards rather than the community's standards.

2. In *Illinois v. Wardlow* 98–1036 (2000) the Supreme Court ruled that if an individual runs in a high crime area, the officer has reasonable suspicion to stop the individual.

3. Sanders (2010) interviewed four chiefs of small police agencies, and these chiefs claimed to not measure officer performance via citations and arrests. Sanders's research, however, is atypical and not reflective of this field in general.

4. "Motors" are traffic division officers on the force who are assigned to enforce the vehicle code.

5. Future research that records the amount of time officers hunt will more thoroughly illustrate this phenomenon. A record of time, as opposed to a record of contacts, will more clearly reveal the extent of proactive work.

6. Because Seaside is a much older city than Stonesville, the local culture was for its residents to use public transportation or to walk instead of driving. Based on Seaside's local culture, and as discussed earlier, its officers were much more inclined to make pedestrian as opposed to vehicle stops.

7. We do not include them here because they could easily identify the city. They are available from the authors.

8. The city has a variety of Asian gangs mostly composed of Hmong and Laotian residents.

9. This study is available from authors' files, but is not directly cited in order to maintain the anonymity of the city.

10. This study is available from authors' file, but is not directly cited in order to maintain the anonymity of the department.

11. A base rate of percent Black or percent Black drivers in an area has been used by many racial profiling studies, although it may not be the most desirable (see Engel, Calnon, and Bernard 2002; Engel and Calnon 2004).

12. This study is available from authors' files.

13. Additionally, in June 2012, the Seattle Police Department had to settle a lawsuit for $150,000 because a police officer was videotaped threatening a man laying face down in the prone position, with the promise that the officer was going to "beat the fucking Mexican piss out of you, homey. You feel me?" Police and city officials later claimed the officer's words were not racist, but instead were being used to control a potential robbery suspect. The man was not related to any of the robberies in the area.

14. See Westneat, Danny. Breaking the code of silence following random gang shootings. *The Seattle Times*, June 2, 2012. http://seattletimes .nwsource.com/html/dannywestneat/2018342525_danny03.html — accessed October 11, 2012.

15. There have been similar findings among Latino populations who felt they were also victims of racial profiling — see Reitzel, Rice, and Piquero 2004; Weitzer and Tuch 2004; Zhao et al. 2011.

16. We use 1990 Census data because the research was conducted in 1999. Furthermore, there has not been a great degree of population change in Stonesville, so 2000 Census data is unlikely to change the results. For Seaside, we used the 2010 Census data.

17. As might be expected, many California cities, unlike some other major U.S. cities, do not have Blacks as their dominant minority. As an example, the U.S. Census 2000 demonstrated that Latinos were the dominant minority in Los Angeles, San Jose, San Diego, and Sacramento, while San Francisco's dominant minority population was Asian and Oakland's was Black. While Latinos are the dominant minority in most California cities, overall there is a greater mix of minorities in California cities than in many cities across the country. So, it is not methodologically sound to separate out each minority group and see how it is correlated with drug arrests when we are primarily interested in un-

derstanding neighborhoods as the level of analysis. Poor neighborhoods often consist of people of many races and ethnicities.

18. Uggen and Kruttschnitt (1998) found dissimilar rates of arrest between Black and White women as well, however, their study revealed that White women had a higher rate of arrest. Our contrary findings may be because we examined arrests for narcotics offenses.

19. See Kinder and Sanders (1996) on how issues of race have become much more subtly conveyed.

20. We observed other officers do the same thing when they knew the name of the individual who they were going to contact.

5. A Vicious Cycle

1. For additional discussion on problems with transitioning from prison to the community see Travis and Visher 2005; Visher et al. 2004; Visher and Travis 2003.

2. We refer to the traditional ideals of rehabilitation here because, as Currie (1990) describes, America has moved to more conservative criminal justice policies that focus on deterrence and punishment rather than rehabilitation.

3. See *Schneckloth v. Bustamonte* (1973), *People v. Woods* (1999), and *U.S. v. Knights* (2001).

4. Not all probationers are on searchable status, but most are.

5. See Sutton (1986) or Gould and Mastrofski (2004) for more on how officers attempt to undermine the Fourth Amendment and how they deal with the warrant process.

6. The Bureau of Justice Statistics has not done a similar study since this one was published.

7. Source is the California Department of Corrections. (2010). *California Department of Corrections and Rehabilitation: Corrections year at a Glance*. CDCR Office of Public and Employee Communications: Sacramento, CA. http://www.cdcr.ca.gov/News/docs/CDCR_Year_At_A_Glance2010.pdf — accessed October 11, 2012.

8. Source is the *Uniform Crime Report*. Federal Bureau of Investigation. U.S. Department of Justice, 2010. http://www.fbi.gov/ucr/ucr.htm — accessed October 11, 2012.

9. See also Wright et al. (1992) and Homey, Osgood, and Marshall (1995).

6. The Future

1. For more discussion on this topic see Fagan et al. 2010; Geller and Fagan 2010; Gelman, Fagan, and Kiss 2007; Golub, Johnson, and Dunlap 2006; 2007; Harcourt and Ludwig 2006, 2007; Johnson et al. 2008; Levine and Small 2008; Provine 2007, 2011; Spitzer 1999.

2. Nationally, from 2000 to 2010 there was an increase of approximately 300,000 state and federal inmates. From 2009 to 2010 there was a national decrease of almost 6,000 inmates. While the recent trend is a decrease of state and federal inmates, over the last 30 years there has been a marked increase (Guerino, Harrison, and Sabol 2011). Additionally, nationwide there was a 1.7 percent decline for those on probation, but a 0.3 percent increase in parolees. In 2010, the total community supervision population (those on probation or parole) decreased for the second straight year (by 1.3 percent), but it was only the second decline in these numbers since 1980.

3. View the report at "Results from the 2010 National Survey on Drug Use and Health: Summary of National Findings." U.S. Department of Health and Human Services, 2010. http://www.oas.samhsa.gov/NSDUH /2k10NSDUH/2k10Results.htm — accessed October 11, 2012.

4. View the report at "Crime in the United States." Federal Bureau of Investigation, 2010. http://www2.fbi.gov/ucr/cius2009/arrests/index .html — accessed October 11, 2012.

5. For a small sample see Engel and Calnon 2004; Miller 2009; Roh and Robinson 2009; Tillyer and Engel 2010; Warren et al. 2006.

6. In Goldstein's 1979 article in which he recommended and outlined problem oriented policing, he recognized that often what citizens want from the police is merely reliable information.

7. Additional information about this case can be found at "ACLU Announces Settlement in "Highway Robbery" Cases in Texas." American Civil Liberties Union, 2012. http://www.aclu.org/criminal-law-reform /aclu-announces-settlement-highway-robbery-cases-texas — accessed October 11, 2012.

8. Additional information about the case can be found at "Racial Profiling: Definition." American Civil Liberties Union, 2005. http://www

.aclu.org/racial-justice/racial-profiling-definition — accessed October 11, 2012.

9. See "2010 Census Shows America's Diversity." U. S. Census Bureau, 2011. http://2010.census.gov/news/releases/operations/cb11-cn125.html — accessed October 11, 2012.

10. Information about the United States Department of Justice case against Sheriff Joe Arpaio was found from several *New York Times* articles: Santos, Fernanda, "Arizona Sheriff's Trial Begins with Focus on Complaints About Illegal Immigrants," *New York Times*, July 19, 2012, http://www.nytimes.com/2012/07/20/us/sheriff-joe-arpaio-trial-opens -in-phoenix.html — accessed October 11, 2012; Santos, Fernanda and Charlie Savage, "Lawsuit Says Sheriff Discriminated Against Latinos," *New York Times*, May 10, 2012, http://www.nytimes.com/2012/05/11/us /justice-department-sues-arizona-sheriff-joe-arpaio.html — accessed October 11, 2012; Rosenthal, Andrew, "Sheriff Joe On Trial," *New York Times*, July 15, 2012, http://www.nytimes.com/2012/07/16/opinion/sheriff-joe-on -trial.html — accessed October 11, 2012; Downes, Lawrence, "Joe Arpaio's American Dream," New York Times, July 24, 2012, http://takingnote .blogs.nytimes.com/2012/07/24/joe-arpaios-american-dream/—accessed October 11, 2012.

11. Additionally, over thirty federal officers working at Boston's Logan International Airport have claimed that they have been encouraged to stop, search, and question potential passengers that fit certain profiles (being Latino and flying to Miami or being Black wearing a backwards baseball cap, which are not terrorist-related and definitely are not illegal; Schmidt and Lichtblau, 2012).

12. Perhaps somewhat ironically, some of the nation's largest police department mottos stress service to the community above all else — for a small sample see the mottos for the following departments: Chicago, Philadelphia, Seattle, and St. Louis.

13. The Minneapolis Domestic Violence Experiment (Sherman and Berk 1984) findings included that when officers arrested the perpetrator, there was a lower rate of repeat violence as compared to when officers used mediation or separation. Replications of the study, however, have called into question whether that holds true for all types of perpetrators.

14. It has historically been very challenging to implement change in police agencies (for a brief discussion see: Angell 1971; Chappell 2009; Goldstein 1987; 1990; Guyot 1979; King 2000; Lurigio and Skogan 1994; Maguire 1997; Patten 2010; Rosenbaum, Yeh, and Wilkinson 1994; Skolnick and Bayley 1986; Steinheider and Wuestewald 2008).

15. See also Wilson (1968) on how administrative and political context affect police behavior.

Abadinsky, Howard. *Discretionary Justice: An Introduction to Discretion in the Criminal Justice System*. Springfield, IL: Thomas Books, 1984.

Abadinsky, Howard. *Probation and Parole-Theory and Practice*. Upper Saddle, New Jersey: Prentice-Hall, 2000.

Abdollahi, M. Katherine. "Understanding Police Stress Research." *Journal of Forensic Psychology Practice* 2 (2002): 1–24.

Alpert, Geoffrey P. "Police Use of Deadly Force: The Miami Experience." In *Critical Issues in Policing: Contemporary Reading*, edited by Roger G. Dunham and Geoffrey P. Alpert, 480–97. Prospect Heights, IL: Waveland Press, 2009.

Alpert, Geoffrey P., and Roger G. Dunham. *Understanding Police Use of Force: Officers, Suspects and Reciprocity*. New York: Cambridge University Press, 2004.

Anderson, Anita S., and Celia C. Lo. "Intimate Partner Violence within Law Enforcement Families." *Journal of Interpersonal Violence* 26 (2011): 1176–1193.

Austin, Roy L., and Mark D. Allen. "Racial Disparity in Arrest Rates as an Explanatory of Racial Disparity in Commitment to Pennsylvania's Prisons." *Journal of Research in Crime and Delinquency* 37 (May 2000): 200–220.

Bannerji, Himani. *Thinking Through: Essays on Feminism, Marxism, and Anti-Racism*. Toronto: Women's Press, 1995.

Barrera, Mario. *Race and Class in the Southwest: A Theory of Racial Inequality*. Notre Dame: University of Notre Dame Press, 1979.

Beck, Allen. "Prisoners in 1999." *Bureau of Justice Statistics Bulletin*. Washington, D.C.: U.S. Department of Justice, NCJ 183476, 2000.

Benedict, Reed, and Lin Huff-Corzine. "Return to the Scene of Punishment: Recidivism of Adult Male Property Offenders on Felony Probation, 1986–1989." *Journal of Research in Crime & Delinquency* 34 (May 1997): 237–252.

Bennett, Trevor, Katy Holloway, and David Farrington. "The Statistical Association Between Drug Misuse and Crime: A Meta-Analysis." *Aggression and Violent Behavior* 13 (2008): 107–118.

Berk, Sarah F., and Donnileen R. Loseke. "'Handling' Family Violence: Situational Determinants of Police Arrest in Domestic Disturbances." *Law and Society Review* 15 (1980–1981): 317–346.

Bittner, Egon. *Aspects of Police Work.* Boston: Northeastern University Press, 1990.

Black, Donald. *The Manners and Customs of the Police.* New York: Academic Press, 1980.

Blumberg, Abraham. "The Power of Police Discretion." In *Criminal Justice: Allies and Adversaries,* edited by John Snortum and Ilana Hadar. Pacific Palisades: Palisades Publishers, 1978.

Bollingmo, Guri C., Ellen O. Wessel, Dag Erik Eilertsen, Svein Magnussen. "Credibility of the Emotional Witness: A Study of Ratings by Police Investigators." *Psychology, Crime & Law* 14 (January 2008): 29–40.

Bolton, Kenneth Jr. "Shared Perceptions: Black Officers Discuss Continuing Barriers in Policing." *Policing: An International Journal of Police Strategies & Management* 26 (2003): 386–399.

Bowers, Kate J., Shane D. Johnson, Rob T. Guerette, Lucia Summers, and Suzanne Poynton. "Spatial Displacement and Diffusion of Benefits among Geographically Focused Policing Initiatives: A Meta-Analytical Review." *Journal of Experimental Criminology* 7 (2011): 347–374.

Boydston, John. *San Diego Field Interrogation: Final Report.* Washington, D.C.: Police Foundation, 1975.

Braga, Anthony A., and Brenda J. Bond. "Policing Crime and Disorder Hot Spots: A Randomized Controlled Trial." *Criminology* 46 (2008): 577–607.

Braga, Anthony A., David M. Hureau, and Andrew V. Papachristos. "An Ex Post Facto Evaluation Framework for Place-Based Police Interventions." *Evaluation Review* 35 (2012): 592–626.

Brandl, Steven G., Meghan S. Stroshine, and James Frank. "Who are the Complaint-Prone Officers? An Examination of the Relationship Between Police Offices' Attributes, Arrest Activity, Assignment, and Citizens' Complaints about Excessive Force." *Journal of Criminal Justice* 29 (2001): 521–529.

Bratton, William, and Peter Knobler. *The Turnaround: How America's Top Cop Reversed the Crime Epidemic*. New York: Random House, 1998.

Brewer, Rose. "Black Women's Economic Inequality: The Intersection of Race Gender and Class." *International Policy Review* 6 (1997.): 46–50.

Broderick, John. *Police in a Time of Change*. Prospect Heights, IL: Waveland Press, 1987.

Brown, Lee P., and Mary Ann Wycoff. "Policing Houston: Reducing Fear and Improving Service." *Crime and Delinquency* 33 (1987): 71–89.

Brown, Michael K. *Working the Street*. New York: Russell Sage Foundation, 1981.

Brown, Richard M. "Vigilante Policing." In *Violence in America: Historical and Comparative Perspectives*, edited by Hugh Davis Graham and Ted Gurr. Washington: SGPO, 1969.

Brown, Robert A., and James Frank. "Race and Officer Decision Making: Examining Differences in Arrest Outcomes between Black and White Officers." *Justice Quarterly* 23 (March 2006): 97–125.

Brown-Barkley, Elsa. "What Has Happened Here: The Politics of Difference in Women's History and Feminist Politics." In *We Specialize in the Wholly Impossible: A Reader in Black Women's History*, edited by Darlene C. Hine, W. King, and L. Reed, 39–54. Brooklyn, NY: Carlson Publishing, 1995.

Buzawa, Eve, and Carl Buzawa. *Domestic Violence the Changing Criminal Justice Response*. Westport, CT: Auburn House, 1992.

Carson, Dale C. *Arrest-Proof Yourself: An Ex-Cop Reveals How Easy It Is for Anyone to Get Arrested, How Even a Single Arrest Could Ruin Your Life, and What to Do If the Police Get in Your Face*. Chicago: Chicago Review Press, 2007.

Carter, William H., Michael Schill, and Susan M. Watcher. "Polarisation, Public Housing, and Racial Minorities in U.S. Cities." *Urban Studies* 35 (1998): 1889–1911.

Chaiken, Jan, Peter Greenwood, and Joan Petersilia. "The Criminal Investigation Process: A Summary Report." *Policy Analysis* 3 (1977): 187–217.

Chambliss, William J. "Policing the Ghetto Underclass: The Politics of Law and Law Enforcement." *Social Problems* 41 (May 1994): 177–194.

Chambliss, William J. *Power, Politics, and Crime.* Boulder, CO: Westview Press, 2001.

Cheurprakobkit, Sutham. "Police-Citizen Contact and Police Performance." *Journal of Criminal Justice* 28 (2000): 325–26.

Choi, Chi, Charles C. Turner, and Craig Volden. "Means, Motive, and Opportunity: Politics, Community Needs, and Community Oriented Policing Services Grants." *American Politics Research* 30 (July 2002): 423–455.

Chu, Doris C., and Linda S.J. Hung, "Chinese Immigrants' Attitude Toward the Police in San Francisco." *Policing: An International Journal of Police Strategies and Management* 33 (2010): 621–643.

Clarke, Stevens, Yuan-Huei Lin, and W. LeAnn Wallace. *Probationer Recidivism in North Carolina: Measurement and Classification of Risk.* Chapel Hill: University of North Carolina, Institute of Government, 1988.

Clear, Todd. *Harm in American Penology: Offenders, Victims and their Communities.* Albany: State University of New York Press, 1994.

Cole, David. *No Equal Justice: Race and Class in the American Criminal Justice System.* New York: The New Press, 1999.

Cole, George, and Christopher Smith. *Criminal Justice in America.* Belmont, CA: Wadsworth Press, 1999.

Conley, Darlene. "Adding Color to a Black and White Picture: Using Qualitative Data to Explain Racial Disproportionality in the Juvenile Justice System." In *Race, Class, Gender, and Justice in the United States,* edited by Charles Reasons, Darlene Conley, and Julius Debro. Boston: Allyn & Bacon, 2002.

Cooper, John. *The Police and the Ghetto.* Port Washington, NY: Kennikat Presss, 1980.

Cordner, Gary, and Elizabeth Perkins Biebel. "Problem-Oriented Policing in Practice." *Criminology and Public Policy* 4 (May 2005): 155–180.

Coulter, Martha L, Kathryn Kuehnle, Robert Byers, and Moya Alfonso. "Police-Reporting Behavior and Victim-Police Interactions as Described by Women in Domestic Violence Shelter." *Journal of Interpersonal Violence* 14 (December 1999): 1290–1298.

Crisp, H. Dean, and R. J. Hines. "COMPSTAT in a Midsize Agency: The COMPSTAT Process in Columbia." *Police Chief* 74 (2007): 46–49.

Cullen, Francis T., Terrence Lemming, Bruce Link, and John F. Wozniak. "The Impact of Social Supports in Police Stress." *Criminology* 23 (August 1985): 503–522.

Currie, Elliot. "Crime, Justice, and the Social Environment." In *The Politics of Law: A Progressive Critique*, edited by David Kairys. New York: Pantheon Books, 1990.

Darensburg, Tahera, Michael E. Andrew, Tara A. Hartley, Cecil M. Burchfiel, Desta Fekedulegn, and John M. Volanti. "Gender and Age Differences in Posttraumatic Stress Disorder and Depression Among Buffalo Police Officers." *Traumatology* 12 (2006): 220–228.

Davis, Kenneth Culp. *Discretionary Justice: A Preliminary Inquiry.* Urbana, IL: University of Illinois Press, 1971.

Dilulio, John. 1995. "Why Violent Crime Rates Have Dropped." *Wall Street Journal,* September 6, 1995, p. A19.

Douthit, Nathan. "August Vollmer, Berkeley's First Chief of Police, and the Emergence of Police Professionalism." *California Historical Quarterly,* LIV (1975): 101–124.

Dowler, Kenneth, and Bruce Arai. "Stress, Gender, and Policing: The Impact of Perceived Gender Discrimination on Symptoms of Stress." *International Journal of Political Science & Management* 10 (2008): 123–135.

Dreyfuss, Robert. "The Cops are Watching You." *The Nation,* June 3, 2002.

Dunn, William C. *Boot: An LAPD Officer's Rookie Year.* New York: iUniverse Inc., 2008.

Elliot, Delbert S. "Criminal Justice Procedures in Family Violence Crimes." In *Crime and Justice,* edited by Michael Tonry and Norval Morris. Chicago: University of Chicago Press, 1989.

Engel, Robin S. "A Critique of the 'Outcome Test' in Racial Profiling Research." *Justice Quarterly* 25 (March 2008): 1–36.

Engel, Robin S., and Eric Silver. "Effects of Supervisory Styles on Patrol Officer Behavior." *Police Quarterly* 3 (2000): 262–93.

Engel, Robin S., and Jennifer M. Calnon. "Comparing Benchmark Methodologies for Police- Citizen Contacts: Traffic Stop Data Collection for the Pennsylvania State Police." *Police Quarterly* 7 (2004): 97–125.

Engel, Robin S., and Jennifer M. Calnon. "Examining the Influence of

Drivers' Characteristics During Traffic Stops with Police: Results from a National Survey." *Justice Quarterly* 21 (2004): 49–90.

Engel, Robin S., Jennifer M. Calnon, and Thomas J. Bernard. "Theory and Racial Profiling: Shortcomings and Future Directions in Research." *Justice Quarterly* 19 (2002): 249–273.

Engel, Robin S., James Sobol, and Robert E. Worden. "Further Exploration of the Demeanor Hypothesis: The Interaction Effects of Suspects' Characteristics and Demeanor on Police Behavior." *Justice Quarterly* 17 (2000): 235–258.

Ervelles, Nirmala. "Disability and the Dialectics of Difference." *Disability & Society* 11 (1996): 519–537.

Estrich, Susan. *Real Rape: How the Legal System Victimizes Women Who Say No.* Cambridge: Harvard University Press, 1987.

Fagan, Jeffrey, and Garth Davies. "Street Stop and Broken Windows: Terry, Race, and Disorder in New York City." *Fodham Urban Law Journal.* 28 (2000) 457–504.

Fagan, Jeffrey, Amanda Geller, Garth Davies, and Valerie West. "Street Stops and Broken Windows Revisited: The Demography and Logic of Proactive Policing in a Safe and Changing City." In *Race, Ethnicity, and Policing: New and Essential Readings,* edited by Stephen K. Rice, and Michael D. White. New York, New York University Press: 2009.

Fagan, Jeffrey, and Tracey L. Meares. "Punishment, Deterrence and Social Control: The Paradox of Punishment in Minority Communities." *Ohio State Journal of Criminal Law* 6 (2008): 173–229.

Famega, Christine N., "Variation in Officer Downtime: A Review of the Research." *Policing: Variation in Officer Downtime: A Review of the Research* 28 (2005): 388–414.

Famega, Christine N., Frank James, and Lorraine Mazerolle. "Managing Police Patrol Time: The Role of Supervisor Directives." *JQ: Justice Quarterly* 22 (2005): 540–559.

Feeley, Malcolm. *The Process is the Punishment: Handling Cases in a Lower Criminal Court.* New York: Russell Sage Foundation, 1979.

Feeley, Malcolm, and Jonathan Simon. "The New Penology: Notes on the Emerging Strategy of Corrections and its Implications." *Criminology* 30 (1992): 449–474.

Fenno, Richard. *Home Style: House Members in Their Districts.* Glenview, IL: Scott Foresman and Company, 1978.

Figart, Deborah. "Gender is More Than a Dummy Variable: Feminist Approaches to Discrimination." *Review of Social Economy* 55 (1996): 1–32.

Finckenauer, James. "Some Factors in Police Discretion and Decision Making." *Journal of Criminal Justice* 4 (1976): 29–46.

Fogelson, Robert. *Big City Police*. Cambridge, MA: Harvard University Press, 1977.

Free, Marvin D. Jr. "Race and Presentencing Decisions in the United States: A Summary and Critique of the Research." *Criminal Justice Review* 27 (2002): 203–232.

Fridell, Lori, Robert Lunney, Drew Diamond, and Bruce Kubu. "Racially Biased Policing: A Principled Response." U.S. Police Executive Research Forum, 2001.

Friedman, Lawrence. *Crime and Punishment in American History*. New York: Basic Books, 1993.

Fyfe, James, David Klinger, and Jeanne Flavin. "Differential Police Treatment of Male-on- Female Spousal Violence." *Criminology* 35 (1997): 455 -473.

Gallup Poll. "Race Relations." Gallup, 2008. http://www.gallup.com /poll/1687/race-relations.aspx.

Garcia, Venessa. "'Difference' in the Police Department: Women, Policing, and 'Doing Gender.'" *Journal of Contemporary Criminal Justice* 19 (2003): 330–344.

Garland, David. *The Culture of Control: Crime and Social Order in Contemporary Society*. Chicago: University of Chicago Press, 2001.

Gau, Jacinta M., and Travis C. Pratt. "Broken Windows or Window Dressing? Citizen's (In) Ability to tell the Difference between Disorder and Crime." *Criminology & Public Policy* 7 (2008): 163–194.

Gay, William, Theodore Schell, and Stephen Schack. *Improving Patrol Productivity*. National Institute of Law Enforcement and Criminal Justice. U.S. Dept. of Justice, 1977.

Geerken, Michael, and Hennessey D. Hayes. "Probation and Parole: Public Risks and the Future of Incarceration Alternatives." *Criminology* 21 (1993): 549–565.

Geller, Amanda, and Jeffrey Fagan. "Pot as Pretext: Marijuana, Race, and the New Disorder in New York City Street Policing." *Journal of Empirical Legal Studies* 7 (December 2010): 591–633.

Gershon, Robyn R. M., Briana Barcoas, Allison N. Canton, Xianbin Li, and David Vlahov. "Mental, Physical, and Behavioral Outcomes Associated with Perceived Work Stress in Police Officers." *Criminal Justice and Behavior* 36 (2009): 275–289.

Gibbons, Don. "The Limits of Punishment as Social Policy." In *Public Policy, Crime, and Criminal Justice,* edited by Barry Hancock and Paul Sharp. Upper Saddle River, NJ: Prentice Hall, 2000.

Glaze, Lauren E., and Thomas P. Bonczar. "Probation and Parole in the United States, 2007 Statistical Tables." U.S. Department of Justice, 2009. http://bjs.ojp.usdoj.gov/content/pub/pdf/ppus07st.pdf.

Glover, Karen S. "Citizenship, Hypersurveillance, and Double-Consciousness: Racial Profiling as Panoptic Governance." *Sociology of Crime, Law, & Deviance* 10 (2008): 241–256.

Goldstein, Herman. "Improving Policing: A Problem Oriented Approach." *Crime and Delinquency* 33 (1979): 6–30.

Goldstein, Herman. *Policing a Free Society.* Cambridge, MA: Ballinger Publishing, 1977.

Goldstein, Joseph. "Police Discretion Not to Invoke the Criminal Process: Low-Visibility Decisions in the Administration of Justice." *Yale Law Journal* 69 (1960): 543–593.

Golub, Andrew, Bruce D. Johnson, and Eloise Dunlap. "The International Implications of Quality-of-Life Policing as Practiced in New York City." *Police Practice and Research* 11 (2010): 17–29.

Golub, Andrew, Bruce D. Johnson, and Eloise Dunlap. "The Race/Ethnicity Disparity in Misdemeanor Marijuana Arrests in New York City." *Criminal Public Policy* 6 (2007): 131–164.

Golub, Andrew, Bruce D. Johnson, and Eloise Dunlap. "Smoking Marijuana in Public: The Spatial and Policy Shift in New York Arrests, 1992–2003." *Harm Reduction Journal* 3 (August 2006): 1–24.

Gould, Jon, and Stephen Mastrofski. *Suspect Searches: Using Constitutional Standards to Assess Police Behavior.* George Mason University. Typescript, 2001.

Green, Jack. "Police and Community Relations: Where Have We Been and Where Are We Going?" In *Critical Issues in Policing,* edited by Roger Dunham and Geoffrey Alpert. Prospect Heights, IL: Waveland Press, Inc., 1989.

Greene, Jack, and Carl Klockars. "What Police Do." In *Thinking About Police: Contemporary Readings,* edited by Carl Klockars and Stephen Mastrofski. Boston: McGraw Hill, 1991.

Greenfield, L. *Measuring the Application and Use of Punishment.* Washington, D.C.: National Institute of Justice, 1981.

Greenleaf, Richard G., Wesley G. Skogan, and Arthur J. Lurigio. "Traffic Stops in the Pacific Northwest: Competing Hypotheses about Racial Disparity." *Journal of Ethnicity in Criminal Justice* 6 (2008): 3–22.

Greenwood, Peter, Jan M. Chaiken, and Joan Petersilia. *Criminal Investigation Process.* Lexington, MA: Lexington Books, 1977.

Grieco, Elizabeth, and Rachel Cassidy. "Overview of Race and Hispanic Origin: Census 2000 Brief." United States Census Bureau, 2001.

Groeneveld, Richard. *Arrest Discretion of Police Officers: The Impact of Varying Organizational Structures.* El Paso, TX: LFB Scholarly Publishing, 2005.

Gromet, Dena M., and John M. Darley. "Punishment and Beyond: Achieving Justice through the Satisfaction of Multiple Goals." *Law & Society Review* 43 (2009): 1–38.

Guerette, Rob T., and Kate J. Bowers. "Assessing the Extent of Crime Displacement and Diffusion of Benefits: A Review of Situational Crime Prevention Evaluations." *Criminology* 47 (2009): 1331–1368.

Halsted, Amy J., Max L. Bromley, and John K. Cochran. "The Effects of Work Orientations on Job Satisfaction Among Sherrifs' Deputies Practicing Community-Oriented Policing." *Policing: An International Journal of Police Strategies and Management* 23 (2000): 82–104.

Harcourt, Richard E., and Jens Ludwig. "Broken Windows: New Evidence from New York City and a Five-City Social Experiment." *The University of Chicago Law Review* 73 (2006): 271–320.

Harcourt, Richard E., and Jens Ludwig. "Reefer Madness: Broken Windows Policing and Misdemeanor Marijuana Arrests in New York City." *Forthcoming in Criminology and Public Policy* (2007): 1–21.

Hadden, Sally. *Slave Patrols: Law and Violence in Virginia and the Carolinas.* Cambridge, MA: Harvard University Press, 2001.

Haller, Mark. "Historical Roots of Police Behavior, Chicago 1890–1925." *Law and Society Review* 10 (1976): 303–323.

Harpold, Joseph A., and Samuel L. Feemster. "Negative Influences of Police Stress." *FBI Law Enforcement Bulletin* 71 (2002): 1–6.

Harr, Robin N. "Factors Affecting the Decision of Police Recruits to 'Drop Out' Of Police Work." *Police Quarterly* 8 (2005): 431–453.

Harris, David. "Driving While Black: Racial Profiling on our Nation's Highways." An American Civil Liberties Union Report, June 1999.

Harrison, Lana, and Joseph Gfroerer. "The Intersection of Drug Use and Criminal Behavior: Results from the National Household Survey on Drug Use." *Crime and Delinquency* 38 (1992): 422–443.

Hawkins, Darnell. "Beyond Anomalies: Rethinking the Conflict Perspective on Race and Criminal Punishment." *Social Forces* 65 (1987): 719–745.

Henriques, Zelma. "African-American Women: The Oppressive Intersection of Gender, Race and Class." *Women & Criminal Justice* 7 (1995): 67–79.

Hepburn, John. "Race and the Decision to Arrest: An Analysis of Warrants Issued." *Journal of Research in Crime and Delinquency* 15 (January 1978): 54–73.

Herbert, Steve. "Police Subculture Revisited." *Criminology* 36 (1998): 355–356.

Hickman, Matthew J. "Democratic Policing: How Would We Know it if We Saw it?" *Race, Ethnicity, and Policing: New and Essential Readings,* edited by Stephen K. Rice and Michael D. White. New York: New York University Press, 2010.

Holstein, James, and Jaber Gubruim. *The Active Interview.* Thousand Oaks, CA: Sage Publications, 1995.

Horney, Julie, D. Wayne Osgood, and Ineke Haen Marshall. "Criminal Careers in the Short Term: Intra-Individual Variability in Crime and Its Relation to Local Life Circumstances." *American Sociological Review* 60 (1995): 655–73.

Horvath, Frank, and Robert T. Meesig. *A National Survey of Police Policies and Practices Regarding the Criminal Investigation Process: Twenty-Five Years after Rand.* East Lansing: Michigan State University, 2001.

Hymes, Robert W., Mary Leinart, Sandra Rowe, and William Rogers. "Acquaintance Rape: The Effects of Race of Victim on White Juror Decisions." *The Journal of Social Psychology* 133 (2001): 627–634.

Ingraham, Chrys. "The Heterosexual Imaginary: Feminist Sociology and Theories of Gender." In *Queer Theory/Sociology,* edited by Steven Seidman. Malden, MA: Blackwell Publishers, 1996.

Irish, James. "Probation and Recidivism: A Study of Probation Adjustment and its Relationship to Post-Probation Outcome for Adult Criminal Offenders." Mineola, NY: Nassau County Probation Department, 1989.

Jacob, Herb. *Urban Justice: Law and Order in American Cities.* Englewood Cliffs, NJ: Prentice-Hall, 1973.

Jackson, Arrick L., and John E. Wade. "Police Perceptions of Social Capital and Sense of Responsibility: An Explanation of Proactive Policing." *An International Journal of Police Strategies and Management* 28 (2005): 49–68.

Jang, Hyunseok, Larry T. Hoover, and Hee-Jong Joo. "An Evaluation of COMPSTAT'S Effect on Crime: The Fort Worth Experience." *Police Quarterly* (2010): 387–412.

Jaynes, Gerald, and Robin Williams, Jr., eds. *A Common Destiny: Blacks and American Society.* Washington, D.C.: National Academy Press, 1989.

Jordan, Jan. "Beyond Belief? Police, Rape and Women's Credibility." *Criminal Justice: International Journal of Policy & Practice* 4 (2004): 29–59.

Johnson, Bruce D., Andrew Golub, Eloise Dunlap, and Stephen J. Stifaneck. "An Analysis of Alternatives to New York City's Current Marijuana Arrest and Detention Policy." *Policing* 31 (2009): 226–250.

Johnson, Bruce D., Andrew Golub, and James McCabe. "The International Implications of Quality-of-Life Policing as Predicted in New York City." *Police Practice and Research* 11 (February 2010): 17–29.

Johnson, Leanor, Michael Todd, and Ganga Subramanian. "Violence in Police Families: Work-Family Spillover." *Journal of Family Violence* 20 (2005): 3–12.

Johnson, Richard R. "Explaining Patrol Officer Drug Arrest Activity through Expectancy Theory." *Policing: An International Journal of Police Strategies and Management* 32 (2009): 6–20.

Juarez, Juan Antonio. *Brotherhood of Corruption: A Cop Breaks Silence on Police Abuse, Brutality, and Racial Profiling.* Chicago: Chicago Review Press, 2004.

Kappeler, Victor E., Richard D. Sluder, and Geoffrey P. Alpert. *Forces of Deviance: Understanding the Dark Side of Policing.* 2nd ed. Chicago: Waveland Press, 1998.

Kelling, George, and Catharine Coles. *Fixing Broken Windows: Restoring and Reducing Crime in Our Communities.* New York: Free Press, 1996.

Kelling, George, Tony Pate, Duane Dieckman, and Charles Brown. *The Kansas City Preventative Patrol Experiment: A Summary Report.* Washington, D.C.: The Police Foundation, 1974.

Kinder, Donald, and Lynn Sanders. *Divided by Color: Racial Politics and Democratic Ideals.* Chicago: University of Chicago Press, 1996.

King, Gary, Robert Keohane, and Sidney Verba. *Designing Social Inquiry: Scientific Inference in Qualitative Research.* Princeton: Princeton University Press, 1994.

King, William R. "Toward a Better Understanding of the Hierarchical Nature of Police Organizations: Conception and Measurement." *Journal of Criminal Justice* 33 (2005): 97–109.

Kipnis, Kenneth. "Criminal Justice and the Negotiated Plea." *Ethics* 86 (1976): 93–106.

Klinger, David A. "More on Demeanor and Arrest in Dade County." *Criminology* 34 (1996): 61–82.

Klockars, Carl. "Jonathan Wild and the Modern Sting." In *History and Crime: Implications for Criminal Justice Policy,* edited by James Incardi and Charles Faupel. Beverly Hills, CA: Sage, 1980.

Kochel, Tammy Rinehart, David B. Wilson, and Stephen D. Mastrofski. "Effect of Suspect Race on Officers' Arrest Decisions." *Criminology* 49 (2011): 473–512.

Kohan, Andrea, and Brian O'Connor. "Police Officer Job Satisfaction in Relation to Mood, Well-Being, and Alcohol Consumption." *The Journal of Psychology* 136 (2002): 307–318.

Kubrin, Charis E., and Eric A. Stewart. "Predicting who Reoffends: The Neglected Role of Neighborhood Context in Recidivism Studies." *Criminology* 44 (2006): 165–197.

LaFree, Gary. "Race and Crime Trends in the United States 1946–1990." In *Ethnicity, Race, and Crime,* edited by Darnell Hawkins. Albany: State University of New York Press, 1995.

Legislative Analyst's Office. "From Cellblocks to Classrooms: Reforming Inmate Education to Improve Public Safety." http://www.lao.ca.gov/2008/crim/inmate_education/inmate_education_021208.aspx

Liederbach, John. "Addressing the 'Elephant in the Living Room': An Observational Study of the Work of Suburban Police." *Policing: An International Journal of Police Strategies and Management* 28 (2005): 415–434.

Liederbach, John, and James Frank. "Policing Mayberry: The Work Routines of Small-Town and Rural Officers." *American Journal of Criminal Justice* 28 (2003): 53–72.

Lin, Ann. *Reform in the Making: The Implementation of Social Policy in the Prison.* Princeton: Princeton University Press, 2000.

Linn, Edith. *Arrest Decisions: What Works for the Officer?* New York: Peter Lang Publishing, 2009.

Lipsky, Michael. *Street-Level Bureaucracy: Dilemmas of the Individual in Public Services.* New York: Russell Sage Foundation, 1980.

Listwan, Shelley Johnson, Jody L. Sundt, Alexander M. Holsinger, and Edward Latessa. "The Effect of Drug Court Programming on Recidivism: The Cincinnati Experience." *Crime & Delinquency* 49 (2003): 389–411.

Loftus, Elizabeth, and Katherine Ketcham. *Witness for the Defense: The Accused, the Eyewitnesses, and the Expert Who Puts Memory on Trial.* New York: St. Martin's, 1991.

Lonsway, Kimberly A. "Tearing Down the Walls: Problems with Consistency, Validity, and Adverse Impact of Physical Agility." *Police Quarterly* 6 (September 2003): 237–277.

Lott, John. "Does a Helping Hand Put Others at Risk?: Affirmative Action, Police Departments, and Crime." *Economic Inquiry* 38 (2000): 239.

Lutze, Faith E., and Megan L. Symons. "The Evolution of Domestic Violence Policy through Masculine Institutions: From Discipline to Protection to Collaborative Empowerment." *Criminology & Public Policy* 2 (2003): 319–329.

Lynch, Michael J., and E. Britt Patterson. *Race and Criminal Justice.* New York: Harrow & Heston, 1991.

MacDonald, Scott, Samantha Wells, and T. Cameron Wild. "Occupational Risk Factors Associated with Alcohol and Drug Problems." *American Journal of Drug and Alcohol Abuse* 25 (1999): 351–369.

MacKenzie, Doris, and Katharine Browning. "The Impact of Probation on the Criminal Activities of Offenders." *Journal of Research in Crime & Delinquency* 36 (1999): 423–453.

Madigan, Lee, and Nancy Gamble. *The Second Rape: Society's Continued Betrayal of the Victim.* New York: Lexington Books, 1989.

Maguire, Ed. *Organizational Structure in American Police Agencies: Context, Complexity, and Control.* Albany: State University of New York Press, 2003.

Maltz, Michael. *Recidivism.* Orlando: Academic Press, 1984.

Manning, Peter K. "The Police: Mandate, Strategies and Appearances." In *Policing: A View from the Street,* edited by Peter Manning and John Van Maanen. Santa Monica, CA: Goodyear, 1978.

Manning, Peter K. "Community Policing." *American Journal of Police* 3 (1984): 205–227.

Maple, Jack, and Chris Mitchell. *The Crime Fighter: How You Can Make Your Community Crime Free.* New York: Broadway Books, 1999.

Marshall, Catherine, and Gretchen Rossman. *Designing Qualitative Research.* Thousand Oaks, CA: Sage Publications, 1995.

Martin, Susan Ehrlich. *Breaking and Entering: Policewomen on Patrol.* Berkeley: University of California Press, 1980.

Marx, Gary. "The New Police Undercover Work." *Urban Life* 8 (1980): 399–446.

Mastrofski, Stephen D. "Community Policing as Reform: A Cautionary Tale." In *Community Policing: Rhetoric or Reality,* edited by Jack Greene and Stephen Mastrofski. New York: Praeger Press, 1988.

Mastrofski, Stephen D. "Controlling Street-Level Police Discretion." *The ANNALS of the American Academy of Political Social Science* 593 (2004): 100–118.

Mastrofski, Stephen D., R. Richard Ritti, and Jeffrey B. Snipes. "Expectancy Theory and Police Productivity in DUI Enforcement." *Law and Society Review* 28 (1994): 113–148.

Mastrofski, Stephen D., Jeffrey B. Snipes, Roger B. Parks, and Christopher D. Maxwell. "The Helping Hand of the Law: Police Control of Citizens on Requests." *Criminology* 38 (November 2000): 307–342.

Mauer, Marc. *Young Black Men and the Criminal Justice System.* Washington, D.C.: The Sentencing Project, 1990.

Mazzerolle, Lorraine, Dennis Rogan, James Frank, Christine Famega, and John E. Eck. "Managing Police Calls to the Police with 911/311 Systems." U.S. National Institute of Justice, 2005.

McCahill, Thomas, Linda Meyer, and Arthur Fischman. *The Aftermath of Rape.* Lexington, MA: Lexington Books, 1979.

McCluskey, John D., Cynthia Perez McCluskey, and Roger Enriquez. "A Comparison of Latino and White Citizen Satisfaction with Police." *Journal of Criminal Justice* 36 (2008): 471–477.

McDonald, Phyllis P. "Implementing COMPSTAT: Critical Points to Consider." *Police Chief* 71 (2004): 33–37.

McNamara, Robert. "The Socialization of the Police." In *Police and Policing: Contemporary Issues,* edited by Dennis Kenney and Robert McNamara. Westport, CT: Praeger, 1999.

Menken, H. L. "Recollections of Notable Cops." In *Thinking about the Police,* edited by Carl Klockars and Stephen Mastrofski. Boston: McGraw Hill, 1955.

Miller, Jerome. *Search and Destroy: African American Males in the Criminal Justice System.* Cambridge: Cambridge University Press, 1996.

Miller, Susan. *Gender and Community Policing: Walking the Talk.* Boston: Northeastern University Press, 1999.

Miller, Wilber. "Police Authority in London and New York City 1830–1870." *Journal of Social History* (Winter 1975): 81–101.

Monkkonen, Eric. "History of the Urban Police." In *Modern Policing,* edited by Michael Tonry and N. Morris. Chicago: University of Chicago Press, 1992.

Monkkonen, Eric H. *Police in Urban America, 1860–1920.* Cambridge: Cambridge University Press, 1981.

Moore, Mark H., and Anthony A. Braga. "Measuring and Improving Police Performance: The Lessons of COMPSTAT and its Progeny." *Policing: An International Journal of Police Strategies and Management* 26 (2003): 439–453.

Moore, Mark H., Robert C. Trojanowicz, and George L. Kelling. "Crime and Policing." *Perspectives on Policing* 2 (June 1988): 1–14.

Moskos, Peter. *Cop in the Hood: My Year Policing Baltimore's Eastern District.* Princeton: Princeton University Press, 2008.

Muir Jr., William Ker. *Police: Streetcorner Politicians.* Chicago: University of Chicago Press, 1977.

Namaste, Ki. "The Politics of Inside/Out: Queer Theory, Poststructuralism, and Sociological Approach to Sexuality." In *Queer Theory/ Sociology,* edited by Steven Seidman. Malden, MA: Blackwell Publishers, 1996.

National Research Council. *Fairness and Effectiveness in Policing.* Washington, D.C.: National Academies Press, 2004.

Neiderhoffer, Arthur. *Behind the Shield: The Police in Urban Society.* Garden City, N.Y.: Doubleday, 1967.

Novak, Kenneth J. "Disparity and Racial Profiling in Traffic Enforcement." *Police Quarterly* 7 (2004): 65–96.

Novak, Kenneth J., Robert A. Brown, and James Frank. "Women on Patrol: An Analysis of Differences in Officer Arrest Behavior." *Policing: An International Journal of Police Strategies & Management* 34 (2011): 566–857.

Oliver, Willard M., and Cecil "Andy" Meier. "Stress in Small Town and Rural Law Enforcement: Testing the Assumptions." *American Journal of Criminal Justice* 29 (2004): 37–56.

Paoline, Eugene A. III. "Shedding Light on Police Culture: An Examination of Officers' Occupational Attitudes." *Police Quarterly* 7 (2004): 205–236.

Paoline, Eugene A. III. "Taking Stock: Toward a Richer Understanding of Police Culture." *Journal of Criminal Justice* 31 (2003): 199–214.

Paoline, Eugene A. III, Stephanie M. Myers, and Robert E. Worden. "Police Culture, Individualism, and Community Policing: Evidence from Two Police Departments." *Justice Quarterly* 17 (2000): 575–605.

Paoline, Eugene A. III, and William Terrill. "Women Police Officers and the Use of Coercion." *Women & Criminal Justice* 15 (2004): 97–119.

Parks, Roger B., Stephen D. Mastrofski, Christina Dejong, and M. Kevin Gray. "How Officers Spend Their Time With the Community." *Justice Quarterly* 16 (September 1999): 483–518.

Parnaby, Patrick F., and Myra Leyden. "Dirty Harry and the Station Queens: A Mertonian Analysis of Police Deviance." *Policing and Society: An International Journal of Research and Policy* 21 (September 2011): 249–264.

Pate, Anthony, and Lorie Fridell. *Police Use of Force: Official Reports, Citizen Complaints and Legal Consequences.* Washington, D.C.: Police Foundation, 1993.

Patten, Ryan. "Policing in the Wild: The Game Wardens' Perspective." *Policing: An International Journal of Police Strategies & Management* 33 (2010): 132–151.

Pelfrey, William V. "The Inchoate Nature of Community Policing: Differences between Community Policing and Traditional Police Officers." *Justice Quarterly* 21 (2004): 579–601.

Petersilia, Joan. "Parole and Prisoner Reentry in the United States." In *Prisons,* edited by Michael Tonry and Joan Petersilia. Chicago: University of Chicago Press, 1999.

Petersilia, Joan. *Probation and Felony Offenders.* Washington, D.C.: U.S. Department of Justice, 1985.

Petersilia, Joan. "Racial Disparities in the Criminal Justice System: A Summary." *Crime and Delinquency* 31 (1985): 15–34.

Petersilia, Joan. "When Prisoners Return to the Community: Political, Economic, and Social Consequences." In *Sentencing and Corrections: Issues for the 21st Century.* National Institute of Justice, 2000.

Petersilia, Joan, Allan Abrahamse, and James Q. Wilson. *Police Performance and Case Attrition.* Santa Monica, CA: Rand, 1987.

Pettit, Becky, and Bruce Western. "Mass Imprisonment and the Life Course: Race and Class Inequality in U.S. Incarceration." *American Sociology Review* 69 (April 2004): 151–169.

Phillips, Scott W., and James Gillham. "Policing Domestic Violence: The Significance of Charging in the Post-Arrest Decision Making of Police Officers." *Partner Abuse* 1 (2010): 200–219.

Pinkele, Carl F., and William C. Louthan, eds. *Discretion, Justice, and Democracy: A Public Policy Perspective.* Ames: Iowa State University Press, 1985.

Piza, Eric L., and Brian A. O'Hara. "Saturation Foot-Patrol in a High-Violence Area: A Quasi- Experimental Evaluation." *Justice Quarterly* (2012): 1–26.

Pogrebin, Mark R., and Eric D. Poole. "Humor in the Briefing Room: A Study of the Strategic Uses of Humor Among Police." *Journal of Contemporary Ethnography* 17 (1988): 183–210.

Poteyeva, Margarita, and Ivan Y. Sun. "Gender Differences in Police Officers' Attitudes: Assessing Current Empirical Evidence." *Journal of Criminal Justice* 37 (2009): 512–522.

Pratt, Travis C., *Addicted to Incarceration: Correction Policy and the Politics of Misinformation in the United States.* Los Angeles: Sage Publications Inc., 2009.

President's Commission on Law Enforcement and Administration of Justice. *Task Force Report: The Police.* Washington, D.C.: U.S. Government Printing Office, 1967.

Price, Barbara Raffel. "Female Police Officers in the United States." In *Policing in Central and Eastern Europe.* College of Police and Security Studies, Slovenia, 1996.

Prottas, Jeffrey Manditch. *People Processing: The Street-Level Bureaucrat in Public Service Bureaucracies.* Lexington, MA: Lexington Books, 1979.

Provine, Doris Marie. "Race and Inequality in the War on Drugs." *The Annual Review of Law and Social Science* 7 (2011): 41–60.

Provine, Doris Marie. *Unequal Under Law: Race in the War on Drugs.* Chicago: University of Chicago Press, 2007.

Rabe-Hemp, Cara E. "POLICEwomen or PoliceWOMEN?: Doing Gender and Police Work." *Feminist Criminology* 4 (2009): 114–129.

Ragin, Charles, and Howard Becker, eds. *What is a Case? Exploring the Foundations of Social Inquiry.* Cambridge: University of Cambridge, 1992.

Ramson, Amy. "Women in Policing: A Success Story." *Women Police* 27 (1993): 15–19.

Ratcliffe, Jerry H., Travis Taniguchi, Elizabeth R. Groff, and Jennifer D. Wood. "The Philadelphia Foot Patrol Experiment: A Randomized Controlled Trial of Police Patrol Effectiveness in Violent Crime Hotspots." *Criminology* 49 (2011): 795–831.

Reasons, Charles, Darlene Conley, and Julius Debro. *Race, Class, Gender, and Justice in the United States.* Boston: Allyn & Bacon, 2002.

Reaves, Brian A., and Matthew J. Hickman. "Data for Individual, State, and Local Agencies with 100 or More Officers." Bureau of Justice Statistics, Law Enforcement Management and Administrative Statistics, 2000. http://bjs.ojp.usdoj.gov/index.cfm?ty=dcdetail&iid=248.

Reisig, Michael D., John D. McCluskey, Stephen D. Mastrofski, and William Terrill. "Suspect Disrespect Toward the Police." *Justice Quarterly* 21 (2004): 241–268.

Reiss, Albert, Jr. *The Police and the Public.* New Haven: Yale University Press, 1971.

Reuter, Peter, and Mark Kleiman. "Risks and Prices: An Economic Analysis of Drug Enforcement." In *Crime and Justice,* edited by Michael Tonry and Norval Morris. Chicago: University of Chicago Press, 1986.

Richardson, Song. "Arrest Efficiency and the Fourth Amendment." *Minnesota Law Review* 95 (2010): 2035–2098.

Riechers, Lisa, and Roy Roberg. "Community Policing: A Critical Review of Underlying Assumptions." *Journal of Police Science and Administration* 17 (1990): 105–114.

Romero, Mary. "Racial Profiling and Immigration Law Enforcement: Rounding Up of Usual Suspects in the Latino Community." *Critical Sociology* 32 (2006): 447–473.

Ruddell, Rick, Matthew O. Thomas, and Ryan Patten. "Examining the Roles of the Police and Private Security Officers in Urban Social Control." *International Journal of Police Science & Management* 13 (2010): 54–69.

Russell, Katheryn. *The Color of Crime: Racial Hoaxes, White Fear, Black Protectionism, Police Harassment, and other Macroaggressions.* New York: New York University Press, 1998.

Sabol, William, William P. Adams, Barbara Parthasarathy, and Yan Yuan. "Offenders Returning to Federal Prison, 1986–97." U.S. Department of Justice. NCJ 182991, 2000.

Saltzman, Janet Chafetz. "Feminist Theory and Sociology: Underutilized Contributions for Mainstream Theory." *Annual Review of Sociology* 23 (1997): 97–120.

Sampson, Robert J., and Stephen W. Raudenbush. "Disorder in Urban Neighborhoods Does it Lead to Crime?" *National Institute of Justice* (February 2001).

Sampson, Robert J., and Stephen W. Raudenbush. "Neighborhoods and Violent Crime: A Multilevel Study of Collective Efficacy." *Sciences* 277 (1997): 918–925.

Sampson, Robert J., and Stephen W. Raudenbush. "Systematic Social Observation of Public Spaces: A New Look at Disorder in Urban Neighborhoods." *American Journal of Sociology* 105 (1999): 603–651.

Sanders, Beth A. "Police Chief Perceptions of Good Policing in Non-Urban Department." *Journal of Crime and Justice* 33 (November 2010): 117–135.

Schafer, Joseph A. "I'm Not Against It In Theory . . . : Global and Specific Community Policing Attitudes." *Policing: An International Journal of Police Strategies & Management* 25 (2002): 669–686.

Schafer, Joseph A., David L. Carter, Andra J. Katz-Bannister, and William M. Wells. "Decision Making in Traffic Stop Encounters: A Multivariate Analysis of Police Behavior." *Police Quarterly* 9 (June 2006): 184–209.

Schafer, Joseph A., Beth M. Huebner, and Timothy S. Bynum. "Citizen Perceptions of Police Services: Race, Neighborhood Context, and Community Policing." *Police Quarterly* 6 (2003): 440–68.

Schuck, Amie M., and Cara Rabe-Hemp. "Women Police: The Use of Force by and Against Female Officers." *Women and Criminal Justice* 16 (2005): 91–117.

Seklecki, Richard, and Rebecca Paynich. "A National Survey of Female Police Officers: An Overview of Findings." *Police Practice and Research* 8 (2007): 17–30.

Sherman, Lawrence W. "Police Crackdowns: Initial and Residual Deterrence." In *Crime and Justice,* edited by Michael Tonry and Norval Morris. Chicago: University of Chicago Press, 1990.

Sherman, Lawrence W., and Richard A. Berk. "The Minneapolis Domestic Violence Experiment." Police Foundation Reports, 1984. http://www.policefoundation.org/pdf/minneapolisdve.pdf .

Sherman, Lawrence W., and David Weisburd. "General Deterrent Effects of Police Patrol in Crime 'Hot Spots': A Randomized, Controlled Trial." *Justice Quarterly* 12 (1995): 625–648.

Simon, Jonathan. *Poor Discipline: Parole and the Social Control of the Underclass, 1890–1990.* Chicago: University of Chicago Press, 1993.

Sims, Barbara, Kathryn E. Scarborough, and Janice Ahmad. "The

Relationship between Police Officers' Attitudes toward Women and Perceptions of Police Models." *Police Quarterly* 6 (2003): 278–298.

Skogan, Wesley G. *Disorder and Decline: Crime and the Spiral of Decay in American Neighborhoods.* Berkeley: University of California Press, 1990.

Skolnick, Jerome. *Justice without Trial: Law Enforcement in Democratic Society.* New York: Macmillan, 1966.

Skolnick, Jerome, and James Fyfe. *Above the Law: Police and the Excessive Use of Force.* New York: The Free Press, 1993.

Slonaker, William M., Ann C. Wendt, and Michael J. Kemper. "Discrimination in the Ranks: An Empirical Study with Recommendations." *Police Quarterly* 4 (September 2001): 289–317.

Smith, Brad W., Kenneth J. Novak, and James Frank. "Community Policing and the Work Routines of Street-Level Officer." *Criminal Justice Review* 26 (November 2001): 17–37.

Smith, Brad W., Kenneth J. Novak, James Frank, and Christopher Lowenkamp. "Explaining Police Officer Discretionary Activity." *Criminal Justice Review* 30 (2005): 325–346.

Smith, Douglas, Christy Visher, and Laura Davidson. "Equity and Discretionary Justice: The Influence of Race on Police Arrest Decisions." *Journal of Criminal Law and Criminology* 75 (1984): 234–249.

Smith, William R., Olena Antonaccio, and Matthew T. Zingraff. "Executive Summary: An Evaluation of Stops and Searches of the Charlotte-Mecklenburg Police Department for the Years 2004 and 2005." 2007. http://charmeck.org/city/charlotte/CMPD/zstorage /Library/Documents/ArbitraryProfilingNCSUExecutiveSummary 20042005Finalo.pdf.

Sorenson, Jonathan, Robert Hope, and Don Stemen. "Racial Disproportionality in State Prison Admissions: Can Regional Variation Be Explained by Differential Arrest Rates?" *Journal of Criminal Justice* 31 (2003): 73–84.

Spano, Richard. "Concerns about Safety, Observer Sex, and the Decision to Arrest: Evidence of Reactivity in a Large-Scale Observational Study of Police." *Criminology* 41 (2003): 909–932.

Spelman, William, and Dale Brown. "Response Time." In *Thinking About the Police,* edited by Carl Klockars and Stephen Mastrofski. Boston: McGraw Hill, 1981.

Spitzer, Eliot. *The New York City Police Department's "Stop and Frisk" Practices.* New York: Attorney General of New York, 1999.

Stamper, Norm. *Breaking Rank: A Top Cop's Expose of the Dark Side of American Policing.* New York: Nation Books, 2005.

Steen, Sara, and Rachel Bandy. "When the Policy Becomes the Problem: Criminal Justice in the New Millennium." *Punishment & Society* 9 (2007): 5–26.

Stein, Arlene, and Ken Plummer. "'I Can't Even Think Straight': 'Queer' Theory and the Missing Sexual Revolution in Sociology." In *Queer Theory/Sociology,* edited by Steven Seidman. Malden, MA: Blackwell Publishers, 1996.

Stanko, Elizabeth Anne. "Missing the Mark? Police Battering." In *Women, Policing and Male Violence,* edited by Jalna Hanmer, Jill Radford, and Elizabeth A. Stanko. London: Routledge & Kegan Paul, 1989.

Sun, Ivan Y. "Policing Domestic Violence: Does Officer Gender Matter?" *Journal of Criminal Justice* 35 (2007): 581–595.

Sunshine, Jason, and Tom R. Tyler. "The Role of Procedural Justice and Legitimacy in Shaping Public Support for Policing." *Law and Society Review* 37 (November 2003): 515–548.

Sutton, Paul. "The Fourth Amendment in Action: An Empirical View of the Search Warrant Process." *Criminal Law Bulletin* 22 (1986): 405–429.

Sykes, Richard E., and John P. Clark. "A Theory of Deference Exchange in Police-Citizen Encounters." *American Journal of Sociology* 81 (1975): 584–600.

Taft, Philip. "Policing the New Immigrant Ghetto." *Police Magazine.* July 1982.

Taylor, Bruce, Christopher Koper, and Daniel Woods. "A Randomized Controlled Trial of Different Policing Strategies at Hot Spots of Violent Crime." *Journal of Experimental Criminology* 7 (2011): 149–181.

Taxman, Faye S. "The Role of Community Supervision in Addressing Reentry from Jails." Virginia Commonwealth University, June 2006.

Telep, Cody W., and David Weisburd. "What is Known About the Effectiveness of Police Practices in Reducing Crime and Disorder?" *Police Quarterly* forthcoming (2012).

Terrell, William, and Eugene A. Paoline III. "Nonarrest Decision Making in Police-Citizen Encounters." *Police Quarterly* 10 (September 2007): 308–331.

Thomas, Matthew O., and Peter F. Burns. "Repairing the Divide: An Investigation of Community Policing and Citizen Attitudes toward the Policy by Race and Ethnicity." *Journal of Ethnicity in Criminal Justice* 3 (2005): 71–89.

Thurman, Jennifer. "Criminal Victimization, 2010." *Bureau of Justice Statistics* (2011).

Tiffin, M. J. *Women in Anglo-American Contemporary Policing.* Fulbright Commission Study, 1995.

Timoney, John F. *Beat Cop to Top Cop: A Tale of Three Cities.* Philadelphia: University of Pennsylvania Press, 2010.

Tonry, Michael. *Malign Neglect: Race, Crime, and Punishment in America.* Oxford: Oxford University Press, 1995.

Travis, Jeremy, and Christy Visher. *Prisoner Reentry and Crime in America.* New York, Cambridge University Press, 2005.

Trice, Harrison, and Janice Beyer. "Changing Organizational Cultures." In *Classics in Organization Theory,* edited by Jay Shafritz and J. Steven Ott. Fort Worth, TX: Hartcourt College Publishers, 2001.

Trojanowicz, Robert, and Bonnie Bucqueroux. *Community Policing: A Contemporary Perspective.* Cincinnati: Anderson Publishing, 1990.

Tyler, Tom R. "Enhancing Police Legitimacy." *The ANNALS of the American Academy of Political and Social Science* 593 (2004): 84–99.

Tyler, Tom R. "Policing in Black and White: Ethnic Group Differences in Trust and Confidence in the Police." *Police Quarterly* 8 (September 2005): 322–342.

Tyler, Tom R., and Jeffrey Fagan. "Legitimacy and Cooperation: Why Do People Help the Police Fight Crime in Their Communities?" *Journal of Criminal Law* (2008): 231–275.

Tyler, Tom R., and Y. J. Huo. *Trust in the Law: Encouraging Public Cooperation with the Police and Courts.* New York: Russell Sage Foundation, 2002.

Tyler, Tom R., and Cheryl J. Wakslak. "Profiling and Police Legitimacy: Procedural Justice, Attributions of Motive, and Acceptance of Police Authority." *Criminology* 42 (2004): 253–281.

Uggen, Christopher, and Candace Kruttschnitt. "Crime in the Breaking: Gender Differences in Desistance." *Law & Society Review* 32 (1998): 339–366.

Ulmer, Jeffrey T. "Intermediate Sanctions: A Comparative Analysis of the Probability and Severity of Recidivism." *Sociological Inquiry* 71 (2001): 164–193.

U.S. Census Bureau. "Proficiency Levels on Selected NAEP Tests for Students in Public Schools, by State: 2007." Elementary and Secondary Education: Technology, Courses, and Test Scores. Statistical Abstract Table 260, 2009. http://www.census.gov/compendia /statab/cats/education.html.

U.S. Department of Health and Human Services. *Results from the 2010 National Survey on Drug Use and Health: Summary of National Findings.* Washington, D.C.: Center for Behavioral Health and Statistics Quality. http://www.oas.samhsa.gov/NSDUH/2k10NSDUH /2k10Results.htm#2.7.

U.S. Department of State: Civil Rights Division. "Investigation of the Seattle Police Department." *Department of Justice Report* (December 16) 2011: 1–67.

U.S. v. Brown. United States District Court, S.D. Indiana, 2004.

Van Maanen, John. "Observations on the Making of Policemen." In *Policing: A View from the Street,* edited by Peter Manning and John Van Maanen. Santa Monica, CA: Goodyear, 1978.

Velde, Richard. "Blacks and Criminal Justice Today." In *Blacks and Criminal Justice,* edited by Charles Owens and Jimmy Bell. Lexington, MA: Lexington Books, 1977.

Vila, Brian, and Cynthia Morris. *The Role of Police in America: A Documentary History.* Westport, CT: Greenwood Press, 1999.

Visher, Christy A., Vera Kachnowski, Nancy La Vigne, and Jeremy Travis. *Baltimore Prisoners' Experiences Returning Home.* Washington, D.C.: Urban Institute, 2004.

Visher, Christy A., and Jeremy Travis. "Transitions from Prison to Community: Understanding Individual Pathways." *Annual Review of Sociology* 29 (2003): 89–113.

Volanti, John M. "Predictors of Police Suicide Ideation." *Suicide and Life Threatening Behavior* 4 (2004): 277–283.

Walker, Samuel. "'Broken Windows' and Fractured History: The Use and Misuse of History in Recent Patrol Analysis." *Justice Quarterly* 1 (1984): 75–90.

Walker, Samuel. *Citizen Review Resource Manual*. Washington, D.C.: Police Executive Research Forum, 1995.

Walker, Samuel. *A Critical History of Police Reform: The Emergence of Professionalization*. Lexington: Lexington Books, 1977.

Walker, Samuel. *Taming the System: the Control of Discretion in Criminal Justice, 1950–1990*. New York: Oxford University Press, 1993.

Walker, Samuel, Cassia Spohn, and Miriam DeLone. *The Color of Justice: Race, Ethnicity, and Crime in America*. Belmont, CA: Wadsworth Publishing, 2000.

Walsh, William. "Patrol Officer Arrest Rates: A Study in the Social Organization of Police Work." *Justice Quarterly* 3 (1986): 271–290.

Walsh, William F., and Gennaro F. Vito. "The Meaning of COMPSTAT: Analysis and Response." *Journal of Contemporary Criminal Justice* 20 (2004): 51–69.

Warren, Patricia, Donald Tomaskovic-Devey, William Smith, Mathew Zingraff, and Marcinda Mason. "Driving While Black: Bias Processes and Racial Disparity in Police Stops." *Criminology* 44 (2006): 709–738.

Watson, Amy C., and Beth Angell. "Applying Procedural Justice Theory to Law Enforcement's Response to Persons with Mental Illness." *Psychiatric Services* 58 (2007): 787–793.

Webb, Vincent J., and Chris E. Marshall. "The Relative Importance of Race and Ethnicity on Citizen Attitudes toward the Police." *American Journal of Police* 14 (1995): 45–66.

Websdale, Neil. *Policing the Poor: From Slave Plantation to Public Housing*. Boston: Northeastern University Press, 2001.

Weidner, Robert R., Richard S. Frase, and Jennifer S. Schultz. "The Impact of Contextual Factors on the Decision to Imprison in Large Urban Jurisdictions: A Multilevel Analysis." *Crime and Delinquency* 51 (2005): 400–424.

Weisburd, David, and John E. Eck. "What Can Police do to Reduce Crime, Disorder, and Fear?" *The Annals of the American Academy of Political and Social Science* 593 (2004): 42–65.

Weisburd, David, and Cynthia Lum. "The Diffusion of Computerized Crime Mapping in Policing: Linking Research and Practice." *Police Practice and Research* 6 (2005): 419–434.

Weisburd, David, Stephen D. Mastrofski, Ann Marie McNally, Rosann Greenspan, and James J. Willis. "Reforming to Preserve: COMPSTAT and Strategic Problem Solving in American Policing." *Criminology & Public Policy* 2 (2003): 421–456.

Weisburd, David, Laura A. Wyckoff, Justin Ready, John E. Eck, Joshua C. Hinkle, and Frank Gajewski. "Does Crime Just Move Around the Corner? A Controlled Study of Spatial Displacement and Diffusion of Crime Control Benefits." *Criminology* 44 (2006): 549–592.

Weiss, Karen G. "'Boys Will Be Boys' and Other Gendered Accounts." *Violence against Women* 15 (2009): 810–834.

Weitzer, Ronald. "Race and Policing in Different Ecological Contexts." In *Race, Ethnicity, and Policing: New and Essential Readings,* edited by Stephen K. Rice and Michael D. White. New York: New York University Press, 2010.

Weitzer, Ronald, and Steven A. Tuch. "Perceptions of Racial Profiling: Race, Class, and Personal Experience." *Criminology* 40 (May 2002): 435.

Weitzer, Ronald, and Steven A. Tuch. "Police-Community Relations in a Majority-Black City." *Journal of Research in Crime and Delinquency* 45 (November 2008): 398–428.

Weitzer, Ronald, and Steven A. Tuch. "Race, Class, and Perceptions of Discrimination by the Police." *Crime & Delinquency* 45 (October 1999): 494–507.

Weitzer, Ronald, and Steven A. Tuch. *Race and Policing in America: Conflict and Reform.* London: Cambridge University Press, 2006.

West, Candace, and Sarah Fenstermaker. "Doing Difference." *Gender and Society* 9 (February 1995): 8–37.

West, Heather C., and William J. Sabol. "Bureau of Justice Statistics: Prison Inmates at Midyear 2008-Statistical Tables." U.S. Department of Justice, Office of Justice Programs. NCJ 225619, 2009. http://bjs.ojp.usdoj.gov/content/pub/pdf/pimo8st.pdf.

Western, Bruce. "Punishment and Inequality in America." *Industrial and Labor Relations Review* 60 (2007): 594–596.

Westley, William A. *Violence and the Police: A Sociological Study of Law, Custom, and Morality.* Boston: MIT Press, 1970.

White, Michael D. "Identifying Good Cops Early: Predicting Recruit Performance in the Academy." *Police Quarterly* 11 (March 2008): 27–49.

Whitehead, John. "The Effectiveness of Felony Probation: Results from an Eastern State." *Justice Quarterly* 8 (1991): 525–43.

Wilbanks, William. *The Myth of a Racist Criminal Justice System.* Monterey, CA: Brooks/Cole, 1987.

Willis, James J., Stephen D. Mastrofski, and Tammy Rinehart Kochel. "Recommendations for Integrating COMPSTAT and Community Policing." *Policing: A Journal of Policy and Practice* 4 (2010): 182–193.

Willis, James J., Stephen D. Mastrofski, and David Weisburd. *COMPSTAT in Practice: An In-Depth Analysis of Three Cities.* Washington, D.C.: The Police Foundation, 2003.

Wilson, James Q. "Do the Police Prevent Crime?" In *Criminal Justice: Allies and Adversaries,* edited by John Snortum and Ilana Hada. Pacific Palisades, CA: Palisades Publishers, 1978.

Wilson, James Q. *Varieties of Police Behavior: The Management of Law and Order in Eight Communities.* Cambridge, MA: Harvard University Press, 1968.

Wilson, James Q., and George Kelling. "Broken Windows: The Police and Neighborhood Safety." *The Atlantic Monthly* (March 1982): 29–37.

Winfree, L. Thomas, Gregory M. Bartku, and George Seibel. "Support for Community Policing Versus Traditional Policing Among Nonmetropolitan Police Officers: A Survey of Four New Mexico Police Departments." *American Journal of Police* 15 (1996): 23–50.

Wintersmith, Robert. *Police and the Black Community.* Lexington, MA: Lexington Books, 1974.

Withrow, Brian L. "When Whren Won't Work: The Effects of a Diminished Capacity to Initiate a Pretextual Stop on Police Officer Behavior." *Police Quarterly* 10 (December 2007): 351–370.

Worden, Alissa Pollitz. "The Attitudes of Women and Men in Policing: Testing Conventional and Contemporary Wisdom." *Criminology* 31 (May 1993): 203–241.

Worden, Robert E. "Situational and Attitudinal Explanations of Police
  Behavior: A Theoretical Reappraisal and Empirical Assessment."
  Law and Society Review 23 (1989): 667–711.
Worden, Robert E., and Robin L. Shepard. "Demeanor, Crime and Po-
  lice Behavior: A Reexamination of the Police Services Study Data."
  Criminology 34 (February 1996): 83–105.
Worrall, John L. "Public Perceptions of Police Efficacy and Image: The
  'Fuzziness' of Support for the Police." *American Journal of Criminal
  Justice* 24 (1999): 47–66.
Wright, Richard, Scott H. Decker, Allison K. Redfern, and Dietrich L.
  Smith. "A Snowball's Chance in Hell: Doing Fieldwork with Active
  Residential Burglars." *Journal of Research in Crime and Delinquency*
  29 (May 1992): 148–61.
Wycoff, Mary. *Community Policing Strategies.* Washington, D.C.:
  National Institute of Justice, 1995.
Xu, Yili, Mora L. Fiedler, and Karl H. Flaming. "Discovering the Im-
  pact of Community Policing: The Broken Windows Thesis, Collec-
  tive Efficacy, and Citizens' Judgment." *Journal of Research in Crime
  and Delinquency* 42 (2005): 147–186.
Zhao, Jihong, Ni He, and Nicholas P. Lovrich. "Predicting the Employ-
  ment of Minority Officers in U.S. Cities: OLS Fixed-Effect Panel
  Model Results for African American and Latino Officers for 1993,
  1996, and 2000." *Journal of Criminal Justice* 33 (2005): 377–386.
Zhao, Jihong Solomon, Yung-Lien Lai, Ling Ren, and Brian Lawton.
  "The Impact of Race/Ethnicity and Quality-of-Life Policing on
  Public Attitudes toward Racially Biased Policing and Traffic Stops."
  Crime and Delinquency (2011): 1–25.

INDEX